AGING ISSUES, HEALTH AND FINANCIAL ALTERNATIVES

OLDER WORKERS NAVIGATING EMPLOYMENT AND RETIREMENT

AGING ISSUES, HEALTH AND FINANCIAL ALTERNATIVES

Additional books in this series can be found on Nova's website under the Series tab.

Additional E-books in this series can be found on Nova's website under the E-books tab.

AGING ISSUES, HEALTH AND FINANCIAL ALTERNATIVES

OLDER WORKERS NAVIGATING EMPLOYMENT AND RETIREMENT

BENJAMIN V. CHASE

EDITOR

Nova Science Publishers, Inc.

New York

For permission to use material from this book please contact us:
Telephone 631-231-7269; Fax 631-231-8175
Web Site: http://www.novapublishers.com

Library of Congress Cataloging-in-Publication Data

Older workers navigating employment and retirement / editor, Benjamin V. Chase.
p. cm.
Includes index.
ISBN 978-1-61470-253-5 (hardcover)
1. Older people--Employment--United States. 2. Age and employment--United States. 3. Age discrimination in employment--United States. I. Chase, Benjamin V.
HD6280.O5385 2011
331.3'980973--dc23

2011022215

Published by Nova Science Publishers, Inc. † New York

CONTENTS

PREFACE

Although the economic recession that began in December 2007 has officially ended, unemployment rates still remain close to 10%. Especially hard hit have been older workers, aged 55 and older, for whom unemployment rates have reached historical highs. A combination of an increase in the number of older individuals re-entering the workforce and a limited number of job openings is responsible for their historically high unemployment rate. There is a significant number of job applicants for many positions, providing potential employers with a much broader pool of applicants. In deciding whom to choose, many employers may view older workers as more costly in terms of both compensation and health care costs relative to younger workers. This book examines the historical trends in unemployment and labor force participation among older workers, the reasons for becoming unemployed, and the duration of their unemployment.

Chapter 1- Although the economic recession that began in December of 2007 has officially ended, unemployment rates still remain close to 10%. Especially hard hit have been older workers, aged 55 and older, for whom unemployment rates have reached historical highs. A combination of an increase in the number of older individuals re-entering the workforce and a limited number of job openings (i.e., weak demand for labor) is responsible for their historically high unemployment rate.

Chapter 2- The United States is projected to experience two major demographic changes that could greatly affect labor markets in the future. The demographic changes are the aging of the U.S. population and the slowdown in population growth. Both are expected to raise the total dependency ratio (the number of younger and older persons relative to the economically productive population). The possibility of a rising ratio has led to concern about the nation's ability to maintain the current standard of living. One way to lessen the dependency ratio's expected increase is for people to spend more years in the labor force.

Chapter 3- Retirement for most older Americans with full-time career jobs is not a one-time, permanent event. Labor force exit is more likely to be a process, as more than one half of all career workers take another job before exiting from the labor force completely.[1] The transitional nature of retirement may be even more pronounced if one considers the impact of re-entry among those who exited the labor force directly from their career jobs.[2] Viewed this way, re-entry may be a form of hidden transitional retirement – some individuals who appear to have exited the labor force directly may in fact expect to re-enter, if necessary. Re-entry may therefore remain an option within retirement, further blurring the distinction between work and leisure later in life. This paper examines the prevalence and determinants of re-entry, or "unretirement," and examines the extent to which the possibility of re-entry is part of the initial retirement decision. To what extent is re-entry viewed as a contingency plan in the face of uncertainty in retirement?

Chapter 4- Older Americans are staying in the labor force longer than prior trends would have predicted and they often change jobs later in life.[1] In fact, the majority of older Americans who have had career jobs make a job transition prior to retirement.[2] These transitions are often within the same occupation or across occupations within wage-and-salary employment. The transition can also be out of wage-and-salary work and into self employment. National statistics show that self employment becomes more prevalent with age,[3] partly because self employment provides older workers with opportunities not found in traditional wage-and-salary jobs, such as hours flexibility and independence. This paper examines the prevalence and determinants of a specific type of self-employment transition – those that serve as a step in the retirement process.

Chapter 5- This report provides an overview of the Age Discrimination in Employment Act (ADEA) and discusses current legal and legislative developments. The ADEA, which prohibits employment discrimination against persons over the age of 40, was enacted "to promote employment of older persons based on their ability rather than age; to prohibit arbitrary age discrimination in employment; [and] to help employers and workers find ways of meeting problems arising from the impact of age on employment."

In: Older Workers Navigating Employment and… ISBN: 978-1-61470-253-5
Editors: Benjamin V. Chase

Chapter 1

OLDER UNEMPLOYED WORKERS FOLLOWING THE RECENT ECONOMIC RECESSION

Janemarie Mulvey

SUMMARY

Although the economic recession that began in December of 2007 has officially ended, unemployment rates still remain close to 10%. Especially hard hit have been older workers, aged 55 and older, for whom unemployment rates have reached historical highs. A combination of an increase in the number of older individuals re-entering the workforce and a limited number of job openings (i.e., weak demand for labor) is responsible for their historically high unemployment rate.

Older unemployed workers face a unique set of challenges, distinct from those of their younger counterparts. The magnitude of these challenges will vary depending on individual circumstances. For example, although age discrimination laws may help older workers retain a job, these laws are less effective for older workers who have become unemployed and are searching for a new job as hiring discrimination cases may be harder to prove than termination cases. Following the recent economic recession, there is a significant number of job applicants for many positions, providing potential employers with a much broader pool of applicants from which to choose. In deciding whom to choose, many employers may view older workers as more costly in terms of both compensation and health care costs relative to younger workers.

Furthermore, most public programs providing income support and health insurance for the unemployed are targeted toward those who have recently lost their jobs (regardless of age). For example, unemployment insurance generally does not provide assistance to the older unemployed who may be returning to the workforce after an extended absence (e.g., retirement). In many cases, their ability to access other resources will depend on their age. For example, some older workers may not be eligible for public programs such as Social Security and Medicare until they reach a certain age. In addition, restrictions on access to retirement savings and home equity under a reverse mortgage are also tied to age. Finally, although the enactment of health care reform will eventually improve access to health insurance coverage for the older unemployed under the age of 65, most of these provisions will not be effective until 2014.

Unemployed older workers also experience longer durations of unemployment compared to younger cohorts. Older workers are unemployed, on average, over five weeks longer than their younger counterparts. About 41% of those aged 55 and older are unemployed for more than one year, compared with 34% of younger workers. Longer durations and less time to replenish lost income before retiring may lead to a less secure future retirement.

This report first looks at historical trends in unemployment and labor force participation among older workers, the reasons for becoming unemployed, and the duration of their unemployment. It then identifies the challenges that certain subgroups of older workers may face and the availability of financial resources and health insurance coverage during their spell of unemployment.

INTRODUCTION

Although the economic recession that began in December of 2007 officially ended in June 2009, it has been a "jobless recovery" with unemployment rates near historical highs. Especially hard hit have been older workers, aged 55 and older. This report first looks at historical trends in unemployment and labor force participation among older workers, the reasons for their unemployment, and the duration of unemployment. It then identifies the challenges that certain subgroups of older workers may face and the availability of financial resources and health insurance coverage during their spell of unemployment.

TRENDS IN UNEMPLOYMENT

Unemployment is defined as not having a job but actively looking for work.[1] The share of those aged 16 and older in the labor force, without a job and actively looking for work equaled the reported unemployment rate of 9.8% in November 2010, a nearly doubling of the 5.0% rate experienced when the recession began in December 2007. Compared with previous years, the unemployment rate for older workers has reached historical highs (see Figure 1). At the same time, unemployment rates for younger workers aged 25 to 54 are similar to levels experienced in 1982 and have not yet reached historical highs.

Younger workers, those aged 25 to 34 years old, generally experience the highest unemployment rates (in absolute terms) during both good and bad economic times. For all age groups under age 65, unemployment rates have more than doubled since the recession began in December of 2007 (see Figure 2).[2]

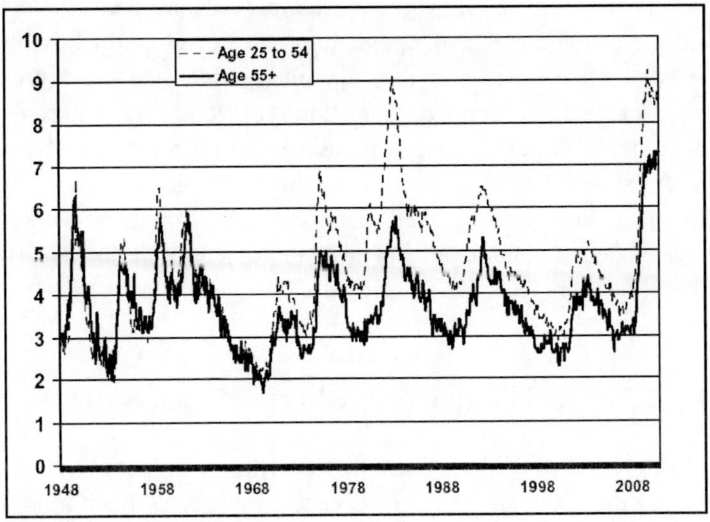

Source: Bureau of Labor Statistics.

Figure 1. Historical Trends in Unemployment Rates January 1948 through November 2010.

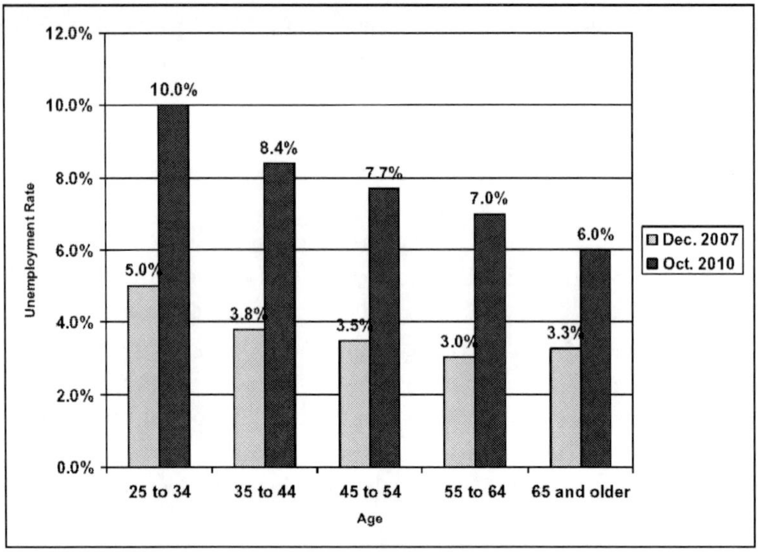

Source: Bureau of Labor Statistics, *Employment Situation Reports* for December 2007 and October 2010.

Figure 2. Unemployment Rates by Age December 2007 and October 2010.

When looking at the unemployment rate, two key numbers are used. The numerator is the number of workers unemployed and actively looking for work and the denominator is the population considered part of the workforce (i.e., the labor force).[3] Since as they age, many older workers retire and exit the labor force, the labor force participation rate (which determines the size of the labor force) becomes an important indicator of unemployment among older workers. As shown below, during the recent economic recession, the reason unemployment rates have reached historical highs for older workers is not only a weak demand for labor but also increased labor force participation among older workers.

Historical Trends in Labor Force Participation Rates

Labor force participation rates for individuals aged 65 and older have varied over time. Over the past few decades, by age 65, the majority of men and women are retired and are no longer considered part of the workforce. In the past, lower labor force participation rates at age 65 among older men most likely reflected the availability of Social Security and Medicare.[4] More recently, however, labor force participation rates for men age 65 and older have begun to slowly reverse their downward trend reflecting: improved health at older ages; jobs that have become less physically demanding; and the elimination of the earnings test for Social Security.[5] In addition, the transition from traditional defined benefit pensions to defined contribution (i.e., 401(k)) plans has left some retirees with lower guaranteed income in retirement, prompting some to delay retirement. Recent survey data support this trend reporting an increasing number of individuals aged 65 and older who still want to work either for financial or non-financial reasons.[6]

Labor force participation rates for older workers aged 55 to 64 have also varied over time. In the 1970s and 1980s, there was an increased trend toward retirement at earlier ages for men in this age group. This most likely was in response to a combination of early retirement incentives in private pensions, and broad access to employer-sponsored retiree health insurance which provided a bridge to Medicare coverage.[7] Unlike men, labor force participation rates of women, actually began to increase during this time period. By the 1990s, labor force participation rates for men aged 55 to 64 began to reverse their downward trend. The reduction in early retirement incentives in traditional defined benefit pensions along with declines in the availability of employer-sponsored retiree health insurance, reduced the financial incentive to retire prior to the age of 65.

Labor Force Participation Rates During the Recent Economic Recession

During the recent economic recession, there were two countervailing forces affecting labor force participation rates among older workers. On the one hand, increased uncertainty in the economy encouraged older workers to delay retirement and remain in the workforce longer. According to the 2010 EBRI Retirement Confidence Survey, nearly one-quarter (24%) of respondents have postponed their planned retirement in the past year. Among the reasons cited for delaying retirement are the poor economy (29%), changes in their employment situation (22%), inadequate finances (16%), and a need to make-up for losses in the stock market (12%).[8]

On the other hand, rising unemployment rates led some workers to become discouraged and stop looking for a job altogether. In the case of older workers, those who became discouraged may have decided to retire earlier than planned and drop out of the workforce altogether and, thus, are no longer counted in the official estimates of the unemployed as evidenced by research on previous recessions.[9]

The net effect of these countervailing forces has been an increase in the labor force participation of older workers since the recession began in December 2007. Among workers aged 55 to 64, labor force participation rates increased 1.5 percentage points between December 2007 and May 2010. For those age 65 and older, they increased 1.0 percentage point. In percentage terms, these represent a 2.3% increase in labor force participation rates for those aged 55 to 64 and a 6.0% increase for those aged 65 and older, over the same time period.[10]

Reasons For Unemployment

The circumstances leading to unemployment vary among individuals. As noted earlier, unemployment is defined as not having a job and *actively* looking for work. Some may be unemployed because they lost their job through permanent or temporary layoffs. Others are considered unemployed and looking for work because they are entering or re-entering the workforce after taking time off to take care of family or to test the waters of retirement. The majority of the unemployed fall in the first category of a job loss. The unemployed aged 55 to 64 experience similar percentages of layoffs as compared with those aged 45 to 54, with about 68% reporting the recent loss of a job as a reason for being unemployed (see Table 1).

The second largest category of unemployed are those individuals entering or re-entering the workforce after an extended absence but are unable to find work (see Table 1). The share of the unemployed falling in this second category is highest among the youngest and oldest cohorts. Within the youngest cohort, there are significant differences by gender. This is not surprising that a higher share of unemployed younger women (42%) are entering or re-entering the labor force as compared to younger men (21%). Census data show that the majority of younger women, aged 25 to 34, exited the workforce initially to care for family, while the majority of men in this same age group had left the workforce after becoming discouraged because they could not find a job. For those aged 65 and older, however, there are no gender differences for those entering or re-entering the workforce as the majority in this age group cite retirement as the main reason why they were not in the workforce initially.[11]

Table 1. Percentage of Unemployed by Reasons for Unemployment, by Age as of October 2010.

	Age 25 to 34	Age 35 to 44	Age 45 to 54	Age 55 to 64	Age 65 and Older
	All Unemployed				
Lost Job	50%	60%	67%	68%	54%
Temporary Lay-off	12	12	12	9	12
Voluntarily Left	8	7	6	5	6
Re-Entrant/New Entrant	30	21	16	18	27
	Men				
Lost Job	59%	68%	73%	70%	55%
Temporary Lay-off	15	14	13	10	11
Voluntarily Left	6	5	4	4	7
Re-Entrant/New Entrant	21	13	10	16	28
	Women				
Lost Job	40%	50%	58%	65%	53%
Temporary Lay-off	8	9	9	7	15
Voluntarily Left	11	9	7	6	5
Re-Entrant/New Entrant	42	31	25	22	27

Source: CRS Analysis of Current Population Survey Monthly Employment Data, October 2010.

Note: Totals may not add to 100% due to rounding.

Table 2. Duration of Unemployment As of October 2010.

	Percent Distribution of Duration						
	[illegible]	[illegible]	[illegible]	[illegible]	[illegible]	[illegible]	[illegible]
	All Unemployed						
Age 25 to 54	17%	20%	16%	14%	34%	37	25
Age 55 and older	12%	16%	16%	15%	41%	44	35
	Men						
Age 25 to 54	17%	19%	15%	14%	36%	39	28
Age 55 and older	13%	15%	16%	14%	42%	45	37
	Women						
Age 25 to 54	16%	21%	17%	13%	32%	36	23
Age 55 and older	11%	17%	17%	16%	40%	44	33

Source: CRS Analysis of Current Population Survey Monthly Employment Data, October 2010.

Finally, and not surprisingly, since jobs still are scarce, the smallest category are persons who become unemployed by voluntarily leaving their employers. Among older workers, this represents those voluntarily retiring. In

October of 2010, 7% of men aged 65 and older voluntarily left, compared to 5% of women in the same age group.

Duration of Unemployment

The older unemployed tend to have longer durations of unemployment, on average, than younger workers. As shown in Table 2, older workers are unemployed, on average, over five weeks longer than their younger counterparts. About 41% of those aged 55 and older are unemployed for more than one year, compared with 34% of younger workers. Both older men and women experience similar durations of unemployment. Among older men, their average duration of unemployment is 45 weeks, compared to 44 weeks on average for older women.

Employment Growth

In Figure 3, employment growth between December 2007 and October 2010 among older cohorts was positive, while for younger cohorts employment growth was negative over the same time period. Looking only at employment growth suggests that older workers are being hired at a faster rate than younger workers. For example, while overall employment growth for those aged 65 and older was 10.9% between December 2007 and October 2010, employment growth for those aged 35 to 44 was a -9.6% during that same time period. However, this statistic does not take into account the aging of the population which means that older workers comprise a growing share of the workforce. One way to disaggregate the effects of an aging population and increased demand for older workers is to look at the growth rates in the *employment-to-population ratio*. As shown in Figure 3, the growth in the employment-to-population ratio since the recession began still shows positive growth among older workers aged 65 and older, at 4.4%, but growth rates become negative for those aged 55 to 64 at -10.4%. Younger cohorts across all ages experience negative growth rates under both measures. Despite positive growth in employment for older workers, the number looking for a job far exceeds overall growth in employment leading to the higher unemployment rates discussed earlier.

CHALLENGES FACING OLDER UNEMPLOYED WORKERS

Workers who become unemployed at older ages may experience a less secure retirement. First, job loss at older ages results in less time to replenish lost income before retirement. Second, those older workers looking for employment are experiencing longer durations as compared with their younger counterparts. Both of these reasons can adversely affect long-run retirement security.

Older unemployed workers face a unique set of challenges, distinct from their younger counterparts. These include age discrimination and difficulty accessing affordable health insurance coverage outside of the employer market. The magnitude of these challenges will vary depending on their individual circumstances. For example, although age discrimination laws may benefit those older workers in retaining a job, these laws are less effective for those older workers who have become unemployed and are searching for a new job. Furthermore, most public programs providing income support and health insurance for the unemployed are targeted toward those who have recently lost their jobs (regardless of age). These programs generally do not provide assistance to the older unemployed who may be returning to the workforce after an extended absence (e.g., retirement). The following discusses these challenges in greater detail.

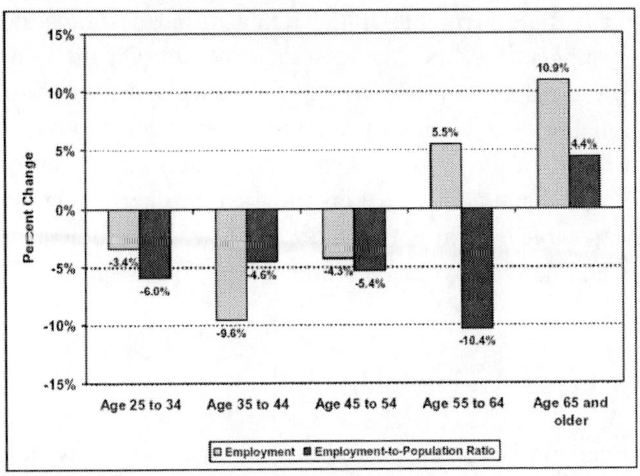

Source: Bureau of Labor Statistics, *Employment Situation,* December 2007 and October 2010.

Figure 3. Alternative Measures of Employment Growth, by Age December 2007 to October 2010.

Older Workers and Job Retention

Studies have found older workers may have an advantage in retaining their jobs as compared to their younger counterparts.[12] This advantage may be due to a combination of longer tenures, age discrimination laws, and perceived positive attributes by employers. For example, longer tenure provides the advantage of seniority when decisions about who to layoff occurs. In addition, workers over the age of 40 are protected against age discrimination practices through the Age Discrimination and Employment Act (ADEA).[13] The ADEA makes it unlawful "to fail or refuse to hire or to discharge any individual or otherwise discriminate against any individual with respect to his compensation, terms, conditions, or privileges of employment, because of such individual's age." Recent data from the Equal Employment Opportunity Commission show that age discrimination claims have risen over the past few years. Merit resolutions, which represent charges with outcomes favorable to the charging party, increased 15.6% between 2007 and 2008.[14] During the same time period, monetary benefits related to age discrimination claims (and excluding those obtained through litigation) increased 26%. Although data recently released for 2009 show some subsiding of these claims, merit resolutions were still 10% above the levels experienced prior to the recession in 2007. [15]

In addition to age discrimination protections, survey data suggest that employers have more favorable attitudes toward older workers in some areas, relative to younger workers, but less so in others. On the one hand, older workers are viewed as more experienced, to have a stronger work ethic, and are more reliable (see Figure 4). Another more recent survey found other positive attributes of older workers, including the need to preserve the firm's intellectual capital and ability to train and mentor others.[16] On the other hand, the employers surveyed did not consider older workers to be as creative or to have as much initiative as younger workers (see Figure 4).

Older Workers Looking for a Job

Older workers looking for a job may face a disadvantage as many employers view older workers more costly in terms of both compensation and health care costs. In terms of compensation, older workers may expect to be paid what they earned at their prior job, which may be a higher wage than younger workers would be willing to accept. Health care costs also increase with age which raises the perceived cost of older workers to potential employers.[17] This differential is even greater for Medicare eligible workers (those over age 65). For these workers, employers are primary payers over Medicare.

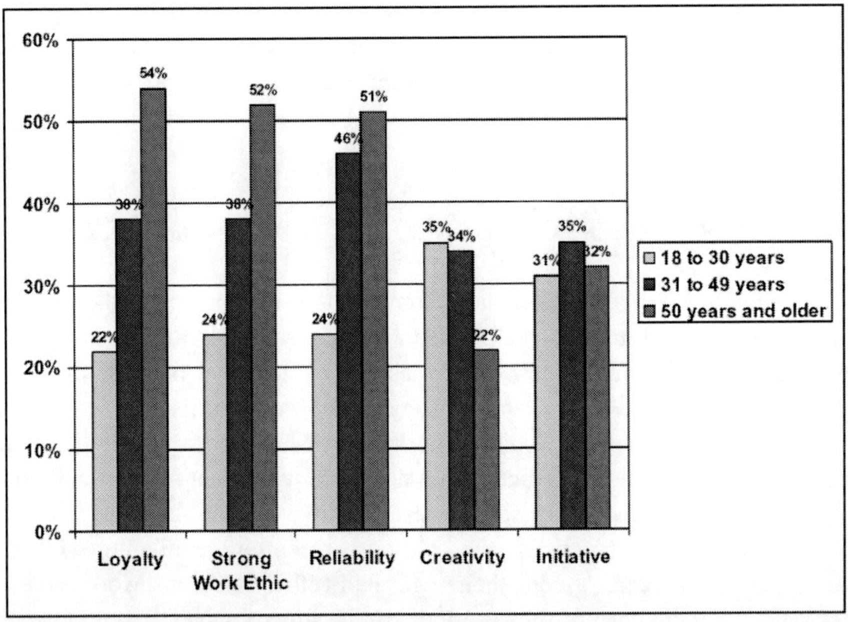

Source: Pitt-Catsouphes, M. Smyer, M. Matz-Costa, C. and Kane, K. *The National Study Report,* (Research Highlight No. 4). Boston College, Center on Aging and Work/Workplace Flexibility, 2007.

Figure 4. Percentage of Employers Attributing Certain Traits to Workers by age.

There are also non-monetary aspects that may discourage employers from hiring older workers, such as the perception noted above that older workers are less creative and have less initiative as compared to their younger counterparts. Also, age discrimination laws may be less effective when it comes to hiring practices of employers. Enforcement data show that ADEA claims tend to focus more on terminations than on hiring practices. Among ADEA-related charges received by the EEOC in 2006, 40% dealt with discrimination in discharge or layoff decisions, whereas only 8% pertained to hiring.[18] Hiring discrimination cases may be harder to prove than termination cases. Thus, these laws may not help those older unemployed re-entering the workforce or those career workers changing occupations.

The empirical research measuring the extent of age discrimination in hiring is mixed. One study found that workers under the age of 50 were 42% more likely to get an interview than those aged 50 and older.[19] Yet, another study found less significant results on the effect of age discrimination laws on hiring.[20] Both of these studies were during a time period when economic activity was stronger and there was strong demand for workers of all ages. As economic activity has slowed, there are numerous job applicants for many positions, providing potential employers with a much broader pool of applicants from which to choose.

RESOURCES AVAILABLE TO OLDER WORKERS

Unemployed older workers have some options to supplement their income and to access affordable health insurance coverage during their spell of unemployment. In many cases, their ability to access these resources will depend on their age. For example, some older workers may be eligible for public programs such as Social Security and Medicare when they reach a certain age. In addition, restrictions on access to retirement savings and home equity under a reverse mortgage are also tied to a certain age. The following section briefly summarizes the various resources available to older unemployed workers given their age and other factors. More detailed information about each of these options can be found in the CRS reports cited under each option.

Financial Resources

Older unemployed workers will have a shorter time period to replenish their lost wage income as compared with their younger counterparts. Available options to supplement their income during a spell of unemployment will depend on their individual circumstances. Those who are involuntarily terminated will face similar options as their younger counterparts, that is, they may be eligible for unemployment compensation.[21] In addition, older workers who have lost their jobs due to adverse trade conditions may be eligible for Re-employment Trade Adjustment Assistance (RTAA). These types of programs, though, only assist workers who recently lost their job and do not apply to those workers re-entering the workforce after an extended period of time.

Table 3. Financial Resources Available to Older Unemployed Workers.

Financial Resources	Source of Funds	Eligibility	Select Features
Retirement Savings[a]	IRAs	Age 59 1/2	• 10% Penalty for early withdrawal before age 59-1/2 unless they meet certain exceptions (e.g., disabled, for health care expenses)
	401(k)	Age 59 ½	• If separated from employer can withdraw without penalty the year in which you turn age 55 • 10% Penalty for early withdrawal before age 55 unless they meet certain exceptions
Social Security Benefits[b]	Early Retirement	Age 62	• Supplements income during period of unemployment • Social Security benefits may be reduced if return to work • Actuarial reduction from full retirement age affects beneficiary and spousal benefits
	Normal (Full) Retirement Benefits	Age 65 (born 1937 to 1958) to Age 67 (born after 1959)	• No earnings penalty if return to work • Benefits are increased for individuals who delay receiving benefits after full retirement age and up to age 70
Access to Home Equity[c]	Reverse Mortgage	Age 62	• Can access home equity and still live in your house • Fees can be high
Re-employment Trade Adjustment Assistance[d]	Wage supplement in lieu of TAA benefits	Aged 50 and older, unemployed due to job loss because of trade reasons	• Encourages older workers to take lower paying jobs because supplement provided equal to half the difference in salary between their old and their new job • Eligibility is limited and only available to small number of unemployed adversely affected by trade disruptions

Source: Congressional Research Service

a. CRS Report R40192, *Early Withdrawals and Required Minimum Distributions in Retirement Accounts: Issues for Congress*, by John J. Topoleski

b. CRS Report R41242, *Social Security Retirement Earnings Test: How Earnings Affect Benefits*, by Dawn Nuschler and Alison M. Shelton

c. CRS Report RL33843, *Reverse Mortgages: Background and Issues*, by Bruce E. Foote

d. CRS Report RS22718, *Trade Adjustment Assistance for Workers (TAA) and Reemployment Trade Adjustment Assistance (RTAA)*, by John J. Topoleski

Older workers between the ages of 55 and 62 who have not worked recently will not have access to unemployment compensation or Social Security benefits and must rely on retirement savings (if they exist), or tap into their home equity. Those older workers who have reached the age of 62 may be eligible for public programs like Social Security, but there are disadvantages to taking Social Security at younger ages. Table 3 summarizes eligibility and the select features of each of these resources.

Health Insurance Coverage

Access to health insurance coverage among older Americans is strongly correlated with full-time employment. Studies have found that, in 2007, 45% of the uninsured aged 55 to 64 have no full-time workers in their households.[22] Recent increases in unemployment of older workers may increase the share of uninsured in this age group.

Similar to the discussion on financial resources, access to health insurance coverage for the unemployed older worker will depend on their individual circumstances. Those under 65 years old and not yet eligible for Medicare may have access to retiree health coverage from their prior employer at full or a subsidized rate, and others may qualify for tax credits for health insurance coverage. Those unable to rely on either of these sources could purchase health insurance in the individual market, which could become costly for older workers especially those with preexisting conditions. Although the recent enactment of health care reform will improve access to health insurance coverage for the older unemployed under the age of 65, most of these provisions will not be effective until 2014 (see discussion below about the Patient Protection and Affordable Care Act). Finally, although the older unemployed over 65 years old most likely have access to Medicare, premiums and cost-sharing can consume a growing share of income over time. Table 4 summarizes potential options available to insuring older unemployed workers or older workers who have left the labor market (e.g., retired).[23]

Table 4. Health Insurance Coverage Available to Older Unemployed Workers.

Health Insurance Coverage	Eligibility	Select Features
Employer-Sponsored Retiree Health Coverage	A vested benefit similar to a pen-sion so must meet age and service requirements specified by former employer	Benefit is becoming less prevalent overtime, less than 1/3 of large employers offer to current retirees High-risk reinsurance program recently implemented provides some financial support to employers providing retiree health coverage[a]
Consolidated Omnibus Budget Reconciliation Act of 1985 (COBRA) Coverage[b]	Involuntarily terminated from employer, employer must be eligible COBRA provider	Premium is 102% of health plan's full premium, could consume a large share of income COBRA coverage often cheaper than coverage purchased in the individual insurance market
Individual Health Insurance Market[c]	Voluntary enrollment	Premiums higher than employer- sponsored market as they vary by age and certain health factors Could purchase a high-eductible health plan to keep premium costs down
Health Coverage Tax Credit[d]	Available to RTAA eligibles as well as individuals aged 55 and older and receiving	A refundable and advanceable tax credit of 80% through February 12, 2011, and 65% thereafter
	a payment from the Pension Benefit Guaranty Corporation (PBGC)	Limited eligibility and must be enrolled in certain qualified health insurance plans
Medicare[e]	Must be age 65 and older	Wide range of benefits, but premiums and cost-sharing for certain services can consume a large share of income Low income elderly are also eligible for Medicaid to supplement premiums, cost-sharing and long-term care services
Medicaid[f]	Low income individuals who also meet certain criteria	Prior to 2014, eligibility criteria limited (over age 65, or pregnant, or have a certain health condition) In 2014 and beyond, eligibility criteria will be expanded

Source: Congressional Research Service

a. CRS Report R41235, *Temporary Federal High Risk Health Insurance Pool Program*, by Mark Newsom

b. CRS Report R40142, *Health Insurance Continuation Coverage Under COBRA*, by Janet Kinzer and Meredith Peterson

c. CRS Report RL32237, *Health Insurance: A Primer*, by Bernadette Fernandez

d. CRS Report RL32620, *Health Coverage Tax Credit*, by Bernadette Fernandez

e. CRS Report R40425, *Medicare Primer*, coordinated by Patricia A. Davis

f. CRS Report RL33202, *Medicaid: A Primer*, by Elicia J. Herz

The Patient Protection and Affordable Health Care Act

In March of 2010, President Obama signed into law H.R. 3590, the Patient Protection and Affordable Care Act (PPACA; P.L. 111-148) and H.R. 4872, the Health Care and Education Reconciliation of 2010 (P.L. 111-152). The reconciliation bill amends provisions in PPACA. The new laws will, among other things, provide immediate reforms to the health insurance market. These provisions are intended to increase consumer access to health insurance, especially for persons with pre-existing conditions and for other higher-risk groups.[24]

PPACA will also provide premium and cost-sharing subsidies for certain eligible individuals, which could include some unemployed individuals.[25] In addition, PPACA will expand Medicaid to non-traditional groups[26] and as noted earlier will cover households earning less than 138% of the federal poverty level, or $20,107 (in 2010) for a two-person family. Beyond the retiree reinsurance program discussed above, these provisions, would not be implemented until 2014 and beyond. This would result in an interim period between enactment of the legislation and the date it becomes operational when unemployed older workers may need assistance.

Acknowledgments

The author would like to thank Linda Levine, Gerry Mayer, and Jody Feder for their comments on earlier drafts of this report.

End Notes

[1] The official Bureau of Labor Statistics unemployment definition is "not having a job, actively looking for work the prior 4 weeks and available to work."

[2] The Bureau of Labor Statistics (BLS) publishes summary tables of the most recent unemployment data each month based on the CPS Monthly Supplement. However, in order to provide greater detail on characteristics of unemployed older workers, the remainder of this report relies on CRS analysis of BLS's monthly data file which lags the published data by one month.

[3] The labor force participation rate is the ratio of employed and unemployed to the total population within a group.

[4] Gary Burtless and Robert A. Moffitt, "The Effect of Social Security Benefits on the Labor Supply of the Aged," in *Retirement and Economic Behavior*, Henry J. Aaron and Gary Burtless, eds., (Brookings Institute, 1984).

[5] R. Johnson, B. Burtrica, and Corina Mommaerts, "Work and Retirement Patterns for the GI Generation, Silent Generation, and Early Boomers: Thirty Years of Change," Retirement Policy Discussion Paper Series, July 2010.

[6] EBRI 2010 Retirement Confidence Survey, March 2010.

[7] See the following: Lynn Karoly and Jeannette Rogowski, "Effects of Access to Post-Retirement Health Insurance on The Decision to Retire Early," *Industrial and Labor Relations Review*, vol. 48, no. 1, October 1994; and James H Stock. and David A. Wise, *Pensions and the Option Value of Work, and Retirement*, Econometrica, vol. 588, 1990.

[8] Employee Benefit Research Institute, *The 2010 Retirement Confidence Survey: Confidence Stabilizing, but Preparations Continue to Erode*, Issue Brief, March 2010.

[9] Till M. Von Wachter, Jae Song, and Joyce Manchester, *Long-Term Earnings Losses Due to Mass Layoffs During the 1982 Recession: An Analysis Using U.S. Administrative Data from 1974 to 2004*, Unpublished Manuscript, Columbia University.

[10] CRS estimate based on analysis the data files from the Monthly Supplement to the Current Population Survey, Bureau of Labor Statistics, December 2007 and May 2010.

[11] CRS analysis of data from the Annual Supplement to the Current Population Survey from Bureau of Labor Statistics, March 2010.

[12] Richard Johnson and Corina Mommaerts, *Age Differences in Job Loss, Job Search, and Reemployment,* Presentation at the 12th Annual Joint Conference of the Retirement Research Consortium, August 5-6, 2010, Washington, D.C.

[13] CRS Report RL34652, *The Age Discrimination in Employment Act (ADEA): A Legal Overview*, by Jody Feder.

[14] Merit resolutions include negotiated settlements, withdrawals with benefits, successful conciliations, and unsuccessful conciliations.

[15] Equal Employment Opportunity Commission, Age Discrimination in Employment Act, FY1997-FY2009, http://www.eeoc.gov/stats/adea.html.

[16] Careerbuilders.com Survey as reported in Plan Sponsor Press Release, *Pre-Retirees Are Asking to Stay On,* July 22, 2009.

[17] Alicia Munnell, Steven Sass, and Mauricio Soto, *Employer Attitudes Toward Older Workers*, Issue Brief: Center for Retirement Research, July 2006.

[18] David Neumark, *The Age Discrimination in Employment Act and the Challenge of Population Aging*, National Bureau of Economic Research, Working Paper 14317, September 2008.

[19] J. Lahey, *Do Older Workers Face Discrimination*?, Center for Retirement Research at Boston College, Issue Brief No. 33, 2005.

[20] S. Adams, *Age Discrimination Legislation and the Employment of Older Workers*, Labor Economics Vol. 11, pp. 219-41, 2004.

[21] CRS Report RS22538, *Unemployment Compensation: The Cornerstone of Income Support for Unemployed Workers*, by Julie M. Whittaker and CRS Report RL33362, *Unemployment Insurance: Available Unemployment Benefits and Legislative Activity*, by Katelin P. Isaacs, Julie M. Whittaker, and Alison M. Shelton.

[22] G. Jacobson, K. Schwartz and T. Neuman, *Health Insurance Coverage for Older Adults*, Kaiser Family Foundation.

[23] CRS Report R40165, *Unemployment and Health Insurance: Current Legislation and Issues*, by Janemarie Mulvey.

[24] See CRS Report R40942, *Private Health Insurance Provisions in the Patient Protection and Affordable Care Act (PPACA)*, by Hinda Chaikind, Bernadette Fernandez, and Mark Newsom.

[25] See CRS Report R41137, *Health Insurance Premium Credits in the Patient Protection and Affordable Care Act (PPACA)*, by Bernadette Fernandez and Thomas Gabe.

[26] Prior to PPACA there were categorical restrictions for Medicaid eligibility. These include the elderly, people with disabilities, members of families with dependent children, and certain other pregnant women and children.

In: Older Workers Navigating Employment and... ISBN: 978-1-61470-253-5
Editors: Benjamin V. Chase

Chapter 2

Older Displaced Workers in the Context of an Aging and Slowly Growing Population

Linda Levine

Summary

The United States is projected to experience two major demographic changes that could greatly affect labor markets in the future. The demographic changes are the aging of the U.S. population and the slowdown in population growth. Both are expected to raise the total dependency ratio (the number of younger and older persons relative to the economically productive population). The possibility of a rising ratio has led to concern about the nation's ability to maintain the current standard of living. One way to lessen the dependency ratio's expected increase is for people to spend more years in the labor force.

Older workers who involuntarily lose long-held jobs through no fault of their own could experience great difficulty delaying their retirement. Older displaced workers usually have labor market outcomes that compare unfavorably with older nondisplaced workers, such as long-lasting lower employment rates. Older workers often are more adversely affected by displacement than younger workers as well. For example, older workers disproportionately end displacement by exiting the labor force than by finding new jobs.

The lower employment rate of older displaced workers appears related to their restricted job opportunities. The limited access of older jobseekers could be due to age discrimination and to lawful considerations of employers (e.g., compensation packages with health insurance). For their part, the likelihood that older displaced workers will earn considerably less upon reemployment dampens their motivation to find new jobs.

Both the Dislocated Worker program of the Workforce Investment Act and Trade Adjustment Assistance (TAA) are designed to actively help eligible displaced workers, regardless of age, find new jobs (e.g., by providing training). In addition, the Alternative Trade Adjustment Assistance program for TAA-eligible older workers offers a wage supplement to those who become quickly reemployed in full-time jobs that pay less than their lost jobs. (A wage supplement sometimes is referred to as wage insurance.) Retraining and wage insurance operate on the supply side. The only federal program that addresses older workers' reemployment difficulties from the demand side is the Senior Community Service Employment Program (Title V of the Older Americans Act). It creates part-time public service jobs for older persons with low incomes and poor job prospects.

To the extent that it is more demand-side than supply-side obstacles that prevent substantial numbers of older displaced workers from obtaining new jobs, raising the Social Security eligibility age may not succeed at delaying retirements among members of this group. Not only might older displaced workers be unable to ameliorate potential labor shortages by extending their working lives, but they also might live in reduced circumstances and qualify for means- tested government benefits as a result of their unplanned retirements. Further, older workers voluntarily retiring from long-held jobs who want to extend their stay in the labor force by taking non-career bridge jobs could be thwarted from doing so by these same demand-side obstacles.

Introduction

The United States is projected to experience two major demographic changes that could substantially affect labor markets in future years. The demographic changes are the aging of the U.S. population and the slowdown in U.S. population growth. Both are expected to raise the total dependency ratio (the number of younger and older persons relative to the economically productive population). The old-age dependency ratio (the number of older persons per 100 individuals in the working-age population) will account for most of the increase.

> Because the rise in the dependency ratio reflects an increase in (generally active) life expectancy, it represents an unmitigated gain in welfare. But to some economists and policymakers, a high dependency ratio raises concerns about how a small workforce will provide for a relatively large number of dependents without a decline in the U.S. standard of living.[1]

At least two means have been suggested to prevent this scenario from coming to fruition. One is that productivity continue increasing at the high average rate attained over the 1960-2000 period. This outcome is possible given the inverse relationship between labor force and productivity growth. Some suggest, however, that the educational attainment of recent immigrants and their offspring might temper future increases in labor quality which helped spur productivity growth in the past. Another possibility is that the labor force will not be as small as anticipated in the future because older members of the population will extend their working lives to reflect the increase in life expectancy.[2]

Healthy older individuals face a number of impediments to spending more years in the labor force, however.[3] Late career employees who involuntarily lose long-held jobs through no fault of their own could also be among those who have the most difficulty delaying retirement.

The ability of older displaced persons to continue working has implications for society beyond mitigating labor shortages. If these workers exhaust any unemployment benefits for which they might be eligible, they presumably will draw down assets including retirement nest eggs. As a result, they might remain in the labor force to restore depleted savings and to reach planned retirement asset values; however, those unable to find new jobs could become eligible for means- tested government assistance (e.g., Food Stamps and Supplemental Security Income). Even older displaced workers who become reemployed—but in jobs with wages substantially below those on their lost jobs—might be unable to save as much as they had intended for their fast-approaching retirements. Thus, they too could eventually qualify for means-tested aid.

This report analyzes the labor market experiences of those older workers who have involuntarily lost long-held jobs for reasons unrelated to their own performance (e.g., veteran factory workers at plants closed because of import competition, experienced information technology workers whose jobs have been outsourced to workers in other countries, and mid-level managers in positions eliminated through corporate restructuring). It examines current policies targeted at the reemployment of older displaced workers which, if successful, might lengthen their stay in the workforce.

THE LABOR MARKET EXPERIENCES OF OLDER DISPLACED WORKERS

There is no single definition of displaced workers or of older workers. Definitions differ by the variables available in surveys and by statute. Shortly after the issue of worker dislocation emerged, the U.S. Bureau of Labor Statistics (BLS) developed the Displaced Worker Supplement (DWS) to the Current Population Survey (CPS) which queries different groups of households over time. Every two years since the mid-1980s, the DWS has been administered with the January or February CPS to determine the number, characteristics, and labor market outcomes of adults who reported that they had lost or left jobs as a result of a plant/company shutdown or move, insufficient work, or position/shift abolished.

In its definition of displaced workers, BLS includes only workers who had worked for their employers for at least three years before being discharged, as they are expected to have greater difficulty becoming reemployed than more recent hires. When utilizing the DWS or other databases, analysts sometimes do not apply a tenure screen. Similarly, some researchers may define older workers as having attained a given age minimum (e.g., at least 40 or 55 years old), while others also set an upper limit (e.g., below age 65) to avoid the complexities introduced by eligibility for public and private retirement benefits.

Begun in 1992, the longitudinal Health Retirement Study (HRS) survey focuses specifically on older individuals, which it defines as persons over the age of 50. Analysts are able to utilize the HRS to examine displacement among older workers because it asks individuals whether their jobs ended as a result of business closings and permanent layoffs (i.e., for reasons other than poor performance).[4]

Researchers have begun to utilize the administrative records of the unemployment insurance (UI) system as well. Its major benefit over survey data is that it offers virtually universal coverage of workers on the payrolls of employers in a given state. Having very large database, even when limiting the analysis to older workers, enables analysts to make detailed estimates (e.g., by industry). In addition, the UI records contain earnings histories over several years, which allows determination of long-term changes in earnings. And, unlike the DWS and HRS, the information in UI records is not self-reported.

The Incidence of Displacement

Just over 900,000 workers aged 55 and older who had at least three years of tenure were displaced during the 2005-2007 period, according to the most recent DWS data. Older persons comprised one in four long-tenured workers displaced between January 2005 and December 2007.

The displacement rate is defined as the share of all employed persons with three or more years of tenure who lost long-held jobs. The relationship between the displacement rate of older workers compared to younger workers has fluctuated over time, according to the DWS data. But, some empirical analyses estimate that the relative rate of displacement among older workers (variously defined) increased from the 1980s to the 1990s.[5] A heightened risk of job loss among older workers may be related to the increase in displacement over time caused by position/shift abolishment. This reason for involuntary job loss is thought to reflect corporate restructuring, which seemingly has taken a heavier toll on experienced (aged 40 to 64) white-collar workers, such as managers, in the more recent period.[6] Other analyses have not uncovered an increase in the risk of displacement among older workers, but because "job tenure, not age, drives displacement trends ... declining job tenure suggests older workers could be more vulnerable in the future."[7]

The Post-Displacement Experience

Older workers typically incur greater adverse consequences than younger workers from displacement according to the measures analyzed below. Those older persons whose jobs are terminated through no fault of their own often have subsequent labor market outcomes that also compare unfavorably with nondisplaced older workers. Explanations for these patterns are presented below as well.

Duration of Unemployment among the Reemployed

A relatively greater number of older than younger displaced workers experience long spells of unemployment before becoming reemployed.

Among those with new jobs in January 2008, 20% of long-tenured displaced workers at least 55 years old had been unemployed for half a year or longer, in contrast with 12% of displaced workers aged 25 through 54.[8] Older displaced workers spend the most time unemployed: At 6.3 weeks without work as of January 2008, this was two weeks beyond the median period among reemployed 25- to 54-year-olds who had been displaced between 2005 and 2007. Reflecting this disparity, a slightly larger share of reemployed older job losers, when compared to prime-age job losers, had exhausted their unemployment insurance benefits.

Two explanations offered for older workers' typically longer duration of unemployment are a greater preference for leisure and more non-labor income. The results of one analysis suggest that this is not the case. Instead, the author estimates that the longer unemployment spells and larger earnings losses of older displaced workers are due more to their inferior job prospects.[9]

The Rate of Reemployment

The displacement of older workers ends with comparatively few finding new jobs. Somewhat more than one-half of long-tenured displaced workers at least 55 years old were reemployed in January 2008, compared to 72.6% of 25- to 54-year-olds. (See column 4 of Table 1.) The group's low reemployment rate was heavily influenced by its oldest members: fewer than one in five displaced workers at least 65 years old who were dismissed between 2005 and 2007 were again working in January 2008.

Further, according to an analysis of 1992-1996 HRS data, older displaced workers subsequently have lower employment rates than a comparable group of older nondisplaced workers due, in part, to the short-lived nature of post-displacement jobs. The disparity in employment rates was estimated to be particularly true of persons in their 60s. The impact of displacement on employment status was found to be long-lasting as well. For example, only 60% of men and 55% of women who lost their jobs at 55 years of age were employed two years later, in contrast with 80% employment rates for nondisplaced workers the same age; there was little narrowing of the employment gap even four years after termination, when the rate among older displaced workers was about 20% less than the rate among their nondisplaced counterparts.[10]

Table 1. Employment Status in January 2008 of Workers Displaced During the Period of 2005-2007, by Age.

Age	Total (000)	Percent Distribution by Employment Status			
		Total	Employed	Unemployed	Not in the Labor Force
Total, 20 years and older	3,641	100.0	67.1	18.0	15.0
20-24 years old	127	100.0	67.5	22.8	9.7
25-54 years old	2,602	100.0	72.6	17.4	10.0
55 years and older	*912*	*100.0*	*51.3*	*18.9*	*29.8*

Source: U.S. Bureau of Labor Statistics, Worker Displacement, 2005-2007, News Release, August 20, 2008..

The lower employment rate of older displaced workers compared to either younger workers or to older nondisplaced workers appears related to the restricted opportunities that older jobseekers typically encounter. Older persons' comparatively limited access to jobs could be due to age discrimination (which is difficult to measure directly because of methodological issues) and to lawful considerations of employers.[11] One study estimated that steep wage profiles,[12] compensation packages with defined benefit pensions, and high demand for computer skills are positively associated with older jobseekers' constrained access to employment (measured by the more concentrated occupational distribution of newly hired older workers compared to younger new-hires and older workers generally). The authors concluded that

> [t]he current structure of the labor market does not appear well suited for later retirement [i.e., longer working lives] given the restricted employment opportunities facing older workers ... who switch jobs, or opportunities that would face non-switching older workers were they to change jobs [e.g., those who want to continue working, but in non-career bridge jobs, after retiring from their long-time employers].[13]

The presence of health benefits in a firm's compensation package also could deter employers from hiring older workers because of their typically above-average health care costs. It sometimes has been argued that if firms are able to make older workers absorb their higher costs by paying them lower wages, the benefit would not be a barrier to reemployment. Based upon an analysis of 1984-2000 DWS data, however, reemployed workers age 55 and older failed to experience greater tradeoffs of wages for health benefits than other displaced workers.[14] Accordingly, another study estimated that employers with health benefit plans have significantly fewer newly hired 55-64 year olds on their payrolls.[15]

U.S. labor markets have demonstrated an enormous capacity for change over the years. Even if firms alter their compensation structures and mix

> in response to the increase in the number of older workers, the legal restrictions on mandatory retirement, the increase in Social Security retirement age, and the declining importance of defined benefit pension plans. ...there is likely to remain a sizable number of older workers facing constrained [employment] opportunities both within and following their long-term career jobs.[16]

Nonparticipation in the Labor Force

Older job losers leave the labor force in numbers disproportionate to their presence in the displaced workers population: While workers age 55 and older comprised one-fourth of all long- tenured workers displaced during 2005-2007, they accounted for one-half of all those who stopped supplying their labor.[17] An analysis of retirees in the 1992-1998 HRS estimated that displacement is one key predictor of involuntary withdrawal from the labor market for older persons.[18] The comparatively long periods of unfruitful job search that older displaced workers engage in, mentioned above, might cause them to conclude that no jobs are available and withdraw from the labor force at a relatively high rate.

The increase in exit rates from the labor force is especially marked among persons 65 or more years old (69.0%).[19] This implies that another contributory factor to labor force withdrawal is age- dependent, namely, eligibility for other sources of income (e.g., Social Security benefits, private pensions, and penalty-free access to Individual Retirement Accounts).

Post-Displacement Compensation

Relatively more older displaced workers who find new full-time jobs earn less than they had on the full-time jobs they lost.[20] Based upon January 2008 data from the DWS, a larger share of long-tenured older workers compared to 25-54 year olds displaced from full-time positions were paid lower wages in their new full-time jobs (43% and 37%, respectively).

> There is a very strong relationship between the change in earnings and tenure on the lost job. The average earnings loss is dramatically larger when the worker had accumulated substantial tenure on the lost job. ... This is consistent with the destruction of job specific human capital when a long-term job ends. The estimates with respect to age, which show a weak relationship with the earnings change, taken together with the estimates with respect to tenure, generally confirm the standard finding that older job losers, who are more likely to have lost a high-tenure job, suffer larger wage declines than do younger workers.[21]

In addition, relatively more workers at least 55 years old who lost long-held full-time jobs between 2005 and 2007 were employed part-time in January 2008.[22] Not only would fewer hours of work be expected to yield smaller paychecks, but also the wage rate of part-time jobs generally is lower than that of full-time jobs.

When part-time and full-time wage and salary workers are considered together, as was done in a study involving data from the 1994-2000 DWS, real (inflation-adjusted) weekly earnings of reemployed workers fell to a greater degree the older the worker. Compared to workers age 20 to 29, real earnings on the subsequent job were 4.2% less among 30-39 year olds; 6.7% less among 40-49 year olds; 7.1% less among 50-59 year olds; and 34.4% less among displaced workers at least 60 years old.[23] In addition, displaced workers continue to earn significantly less than they would have had they not been discharged for up to 10-12 years after termination.[24] For some workers displaced in their 50s, then, the period of reduced earnings could last for all their remaining years in the labor force.

The reason for which older workers leave their jobs affects the degree of earnings loss they incur. A study that utilized HRS data on workers between 45 and 75 years old who changed employers in the 1986-2004 period estimated that wages of reemployed retirees and displaced workers fell much more than the wages of older workers who quit or left their jobs for other reasons (e.g., relocation, poor health and disability, and family or child care responsibilities).[25] In the case of older displaced workers, specifically, pay cuts averaged 12%. Older males who held the job they lost for 10 or more years were estimated to experience an especially large drop in average earnings upon reemployment (20%). The substantial wage losses of older workers who were laid off from long-held jobs could be partly related to the large proportion that found new jobs in different industry groups (60%) where their skills might not be as highly prized. In addition, it was determined that two in five older men displaced from jobs in which they had worked for more than 10 years no longer had pension coverage upon reemployment.

A study that utilized UI administrative records for the state of Connecticut provides confirmation that older (40 and over) displaced workers who change industries upon reemployment suffer an especially large decrease in earnings. An older worker who lost a job in the auto manufacturing industry, for example, and accepted a new job in a nonmanufacturing industry experienced the largest decrease in earnings. This reflects the substantial impact on earnings of the loss of firm- specific skills for displaced factory workers. The researchers also compared the experiences of older workers who found new jobs after being displaced in mass layoffs (defined as an employment cut of 30% or more at the firms that let them go) between 1999 and 2004 with a comparable age group of workers continuously employed over the period. They estimated that earnings losses were larger the older the displaced worker was.

Overlaid on their sharply lower earnings and pension coverage is a marked decrease in additions to the value of pension benefits. According to an analysis of 1992-1998 HRS data that examined individuals aged 50-75, the gain in pension wealth from delaying retirement is significantly reduced for older displaced males.[26] (For older women, the decrease is not statistically significant.) The lower earnings, estimated to be 41% for men and 38% for women, in combination with this reduced "pension gain" were found to significantly dampen the motivation to find another job after displacement. Changes in wages and pension accumulations, however, were estimated to explain very little of the substantially higher rate of retirement among older displaced workers compared to older nondisplaced workers. While some older displaced workers may be unwilling to accept new jobs that pay considerably less than their former jobs, many more may retire because they are unable to obtain new jobs. The study's results suggest that, compared to changes in wages and pension-related financial considerations, other obstacles to reemployment may better explain the high retirement rates of older displaced workers (e.g., employer reluctance to train older individuals and age discrimination).

POLICY RESPONSES

The Dislocated Worker program under Title I of the Workforce Investment Act (WIA) and the Trade Adjustment Assistance (TAA) program are meant to help displaced workers obtain new employment by providing job search assistance and training among other services. Those eligible for the Dislocated Worker program are more broadly defined than the group examined in this report.[27] The TAA program, in contrast, is limited to workers who have lost jobs due to imports of articles that compete with U.S.-produced goods and to shifts of production outside the United States.

Retraining

The WIA program does not reserve a portion of its funding for older displaced workers. Similarly, TAA does not distinguish between older and other displaced workers, but as an entitlement program, any TAA-eligible older worker would be assured of receiving services if they chose to. The TAA program also provides reemployment assistance beyond that offered under WIA's Dislocated Worker program (e.g., relocation allowances).

In effect, WIA and TAA attempt to keep older displaced workers in the labor force by addressing some of the reemployment barriers and financial disincentives discussed above. In light of employer reluctance to train older workers (either because of the short time period in which to recoup their investment or because of stereotyping), the programs draw upon public funds to do so. To the extent that employers' high demand for up-to-date computer skills limits older workers' access to jobs, the provision of such training through WIA and TAA could expand older workers' job opportunities. Training may thus serve a purpose beyond the human capital investment motive of raising workers' skill levels to increase post-displacement wages. However, taxpayer subsidized training does not come with the guarantee of a job at its end.

Fairly few evaluations have been conducted of training programs for displaced workers. Of the displaced worker programs that have been examined, some provided more job search assistance than retraining, solely provided reemployment bonuses, or had methodological shortcomings (e.g., insufficient follow-up periods and failure to differentiate types of training).[28]

Wage Insurance

Publicly subsidized training is in one sense intended to compensate workers for the persistent impact on employment and earnings of job loss that is a regularly occurring byproduct of labor market adaptation to economic change (e.g., dissemination of technological and other innovations in the workplace, heightened international competition in provision of goods and services). By contrast, unemployment insurance (UI) only compensates displaced workers during the period of job search; it neither motivates them to find new jobs nor insulates them from the extended effect of displacement on employment and wages. Recognizing that the nation's UI system provides only short-term compensation and that retraining may not be the optimal solution for all displaced workers,[29] some analysts have recommended that experienced workers who lose jobs for reasons unrelated to their performance receive a supplement if the earnings on their post-displacement jobs are less than on their pre-displacement jobs. (A wage supplement is sometimes referred to as wage insurance.)

In the Trade Act of 2002, Congress established a five-year demonstration program specifically for older workers eligible for the TAA program—the Alternative Trade Adjustment Assistance (ATAA) program—which allows eligible workers at least 50 years old to receive an earnings supplement for two years. To obtain the supplement workers must, within 26 weeks of job loss, take a full-time position with wages below those of their former jobs; the new job must pay less than $50,000 as well. The supplement, which is funded from the Federal Unemployment Account, equals 50% of the difference between the wages on the old and new jobs, up to a maximum of $10,000 over the two-year period of receipt.[30]

According to its proponents, wage insurance might enhance the reemployment prospects of displaced workers by prompting them to consider even those positions that pay substantially less than the jobs they lost. During their initial period of employment, these workers also might have the opportunity to receive on-the-job training that makes them more productive and qualifies them for pay increases which narrow the gap between their pre- and post-displacement wages by the end of their eligibility for wage supplements. If the supplement is available for a limited time from the date of job loss, the payment also could encourage speedier reemployment because its value effectively declines the longer unemployment continues. Thus, in addition to enabling displaced workers to remain in the labor force, a wage insurance program might reduce UI costs.

Based upon the extremely limited evidence available thus far, the actual benefits of a wage insurance program appear to be extremely modest. The Canadian Earnings Supplement Project was conducted from July 1995 to October 1998 to estimate whether the availability of a pay supplement promoted and sped reemployment of displaced workers eligible for unemployment benefits.[31] The two-year supplement was designed to replace 75% of the earnings loss of a displaced worker (up to $250 per week) who found a new, lower paying, full-time (30 hours a week) job within a 26-week period. Displaced workers were randomly assigned to a group that was offered the supplement and to a group that was not. *The low take-up rate*—about 20% of supplement group members received payments—*largely reflects an inability to quickly find new full-time jobs.* The availability of a supplement was not found to affect the timing or intensity of job search among supplement versus control group members. (The only statistically significant impact on job search was to prompt a few displaced workers to consider a broader range of jobs.) Absent speedier reemployment of supplement over control group members, then, the program did not lower unemployment insurance costs. Although the program was estimated to produce a small, statistically significant difference in the full-time reemployment rate of supplement compared to control group members, the difference occurred toward the end of the period during which jobseekers were eligible for the supplement. This difference in full-time reemployment rates—4.4 percentage points at its widest—was found to gradually diminish; by one year after the workers had been assigned to the supplement and control groups, their full-time reemployment rates essentially were and remained the same. The program's most noticeable effect was on the compensation of the few supplement recipients: The supplement, which averaged $8,705 over 64 weeks, represented a large portion of the incomes of these individuals.

Some information is available on the experience of older displaced workers (age 55 and above) who were included in the Canadian Earnings Supplement Project.[32] The researchers estimated that age was one of the primary determinants of reemployment during jobseekers' eligibility for the supplement: Each additional year of age lowered, by about one percent, the likelihood of finding a full-time position. Workers with long tenure at their employers, who tend to be at the older end of the age spectrum, also were found to have a reduced probability of reemployment during the eligibility period. Full-time reemployment rates did not differ significantly between supplement and control group members age 55 and older.

As to the U.S. experience with the ATAA program, it thus far appears hampered by implementation problems that may have dampened worker access to wage supplements. The demonstration went into effect in August 2003, but a majority of states reported various difficulties (e.g., creating payment systems separate from their existing UI check-issuing systems and tardy guidance from the U.S. Department of Labor). As a result, only 19 states had the wage insurance program up and running in 2003.[33]

It should be kept in mind that wage insurance and training operate on the supply side. They do not address the demand-side barriers to reemployment discussed above. The only federal program that focuses on the seemingly limited job opportunities of older unemployed workers is the Senior Community Service Employment Program (SCSEP), Title V of the Older Americans Act. It creates part-time public service jobs for persons aged 55 and older who have low incomes and poor employment prospects.[34]

To the extent that demand-side rather than supply-side obstacles prevent substantial numbers of older displaced workers from obtaining new jobs, then raising the eligibility age of Social Security may not succeed at delaying retirements among members of this group. Not only might older displaced workers be unable to ameliorate potential shortages by extending their working lives, but they also might live in reduced circumstances and qualify for means-tested government benefits as a result of their unplanned retirements. Further, older workers voluntarily retiring from long-held jobs who want to extend their stay in the labor force by taking non-career (bridge) jobs could be thwarted from doing so by these same demand-side obstacles.

End Notes

[1] Jane Sneddon Little and Robert K. Triest, "The Impact of Demographic Change on U.S. Labor Markets," *New England Economic Review*, first quarter 2002, p. 53.

[2] For an analysis of these possibilities, see CRS Report RL33661, *Retiring Baby-Boomers = A Labor Shortage?*, by Linda Levine.

[3] For further information see CRS Report RL3 0629, *Older Workers: Employment and Retirement Trends*, by Patrick Purcell; and CRS Report RL32757, *Unemployment and Older Workers*, by Julie M. Whittaker.

[4] Possible responses in the HRS to how a job ended are: business closed, laid off or let go, quit, retired, temporary layoff, and wanted a better job. Although the permanently laid off individuals often counted as displaced in analyses that utilize the HRS include some persons who may have been let go for cause, their inclusion does not appear to affect studies' results.

[5] See, for example, Daniel Rodriguez and Madeline Zavodny, "Changes in the Age and Education Profile of Displaced Workers, "*Industrial and Labor Relations Review*, vol. 56, no. 3, April 2003.

[6] Henry S. Farber, *Job Loss in the United States, 1981-2001*, Working Paper #471, Princeton University, Industrial Relations Section, May 22, 2003. (Hereafter cited as Farber, *Job Loss in the United States*.)

[7] Alicia H. Munnell, Steven Sass, Nauricio Soto, and Natalia Zhivan, *Do Older Workers Face Greater Risk of Displacement?*, Center for Retirement Research at Boston College Issue Brief No. 53, September 2006, p. 7.

[8] Unpublished data from the Displaced Worker Supplement, 2005-2007.

[9] Todd E. Elder, "Reemployment Patterns of Older Displaced Workers," June 2004 paper prepared for a Federal Reserve Bank of Chicago and the Joyce Foundation conference (Job Loss: Causes, Consequences, and Policy Responses) in November 2004.

[10] Sewin Chan and Ann Huff Stevens, "Job Loss and Employment Patterns of Older Workers," *Journal of Labor Economics*, April 2001, vol. 19, no. 2.

[11] Robert J. Samuelson, "Retirement at 70 (Cont'd)," *The Washington Post*, August 24, 2005.

[12] Oftentimes, earnings increase as a worker's experience at a firm or in the labor force lengthens. The rate of earnings growth (i.e., steepness of the wage-experience profile) partly reflects past education and skill development as well as deferred pay, such that the wages of senior (typically older) employees increase to a greater degree than their current contribution to productivity. Barry T. Hirsch, David A. Macpherson, and Melissa A. Hardy, "Occupational Age Structure and Access for Older Workers," *Industrial and Labor Relations Review*, April 2000, vol. 53, no. 3. (Hereafter cited as Hirsch, et al., *Occupational Age Structure and Access for Older Workers*.)

[13] Ibid., p. 416.

[14] Kosali Ilayperuma Simon, "Displaced Workers and Employer-Provided Health Insurance: Evidence of a Wage/Fringe Benefit Tradeoff?" *International Journal of Health Care Finance and Economics*, September-December 2001, vol. 1, no. 3-4.

[15] Frank A. Scott, Mack C. Berger, and John E. Garen, "Do Health Insurance and Pension Costs Reduce the Job Opportunities of Older Workers?" *Industrial and Labor Relations Review*, July 1995, vol. 48, no. 4.

[16] Hirsch, et al., *Occupational Age Structure and Access for Older Workers*, p. 416.

[17] U.S. Bureau of Labor Statistics, "Worker Displacement, 2005-2007," press release, August 20, 2008.

[18] Maximiliane E. Szinovacz and Adam Davey, "Predictors of Perceptions of Involuntary Retirement," *The Gerontologist*, February 2005.

[19] U.S. Bureau of Labor Statistics, "Worker Displacement, 2005-2007," press release, August 20, 2008.

[20] The BLS definition of full-time employment is 35 or more hours per week.

[21] Farber, *Job Loss in the United States*, p. 25.

[22] Unpublished data from the Displaced Worker Supplement, 2005-2007.

[23] David A. Macpherson and Michael J. Piette, "Do Terminated Employees Catch Up? Evidence from the Displaced Workers Survey," *Journal of Forensic Economics*, 2003, vol. 16, no. 2.

[24] Thomas N. Daymont, "The Effects of Displacement on Post-Displacement Earnings," *Journal of Legal Economics*, winter 200 1/2002, vol. 11, no. 3.

[25] Richard W. Johnson and Janette Kawachi, "Job Changes at Older Ages: Effects on Wages, Benefits, and Other Job Attributes," Center for Retirement Research at Boston College, February 2007.

[26] Sewin Chan and Ann H. Stevens, "How Does Job Loss Affect the Timing of Retirement?" *Contributions to Economic Analysis & Policy*, 2004, vol. 3, no. 1.

[27] The WIA's definition of dislocated workers includes not only (1) employees who have been laid off or whose employers have announced an impending layoff or facility closing and who are unlikely to return to their prior industries or occupations, but also (2) self-employed persons (e.g., farmers, ranchers, and fishermen) who have lost their livelihood due to general economic conditions or natural disasters in their communities, and (3) displaced homemakers (i.e., persons who provide unpaid services in the home to family members, who no longer are supported by other family members, and who are unemployed, underemployed, or having difficulty finding or upgrading employment).

[28] Louis S. Jacobson, Robert LaLonde, and Daniel Sullivan, "Is Retraining Displaced Workers a Good Investment?" *Federal Reserve Bank of Chicago Economic Perspectives*, 2005, second quarter.

[29] As noted by Lori G. Kletzer, "Trade-related Job Loss and Wage Insurance: a Synthetic Review," *Review of International Economics*, vol. 12, no. 5, 2004, p. 740, displaced

manufacturing workers "are older, less formally educated, and more tenured than displaced nonmanufacturing workers. Generally, these are not the characteristics of workers who succeed in training programs."

[30] For more information see CRS Report RS2271 8, *Trade Adjustment Assistance for Workers (TAA) and Reemployment Trade Adjustment Assistance (RTAA)*, by John J. Topoleski.

[31] Howard S. Bloom, Saul Schwartz, Susanna Lui-Gurr, and Suk-Won Lee, "Testing a Financial Incentive to Promote Re-Employment Among Displaced Workers: The Canadian Earnings Supplement Project (ESP)," *Journal of Policy Analysis and Management*, summer 2001, vol. 20, no. 3.

[32] Howard S. Bloom, Saul Schwartz, Susanna Lui-Gurr, and Suk-Won Lee, *Testing a Reemployment Incentive for Displaced Workers: The Earnings Supplement Project*, Social Research and Demonstration Corporation, May 1999.

[33] As further reported by the U.S. Government Accountability Office (*Trade Adjustment Assistance: Reforms Have Accelerated Training Enrollment, but Implementation Challenges Remain*, GAO-04-1012, September 2004), most other states expected to have the supplement demonstration functioning by spring 2004. See also David Wessel, "Aid to Workers Hurt by Trade Comes in Trickle," *The Wall Street Journal*, August 11, 2005.

[34] For additional information on SCSEP and the Older Americans Act see CRS Report RL33880, *Older Americans Act (OAA) Funding*, by Angela Napili.

In: Older Workers Navigating Employment and... ISBN: 978-1-61470-253-5
Editors: Benjamin V. Chase

Chapter 3

THE ROLE OF RE-ENTRY IN THE RETIREMENT PROCESS

U.S. Bureau of Labor Statistics

ABSTRACT

To what extent do older Americans re-enter the labor force after an initial exit and what drives these "unretirement" decisions? Retirement for most older Americans with full-time career jobs is not a one-time, permanent event. Labor force exit is more likely to be a process. Prior studies have found that between one half and two thirds of career workers take at least one other job before exiting from the labor force completely. The transitional nature of retirement may be even more pronounced when considering the impact of re-entry. This paper examines the extent to which older Americans with career jobs re-entered the labor force. The analysis is based on data from the Health and Retirement Study (HRS), an ongoing, longitudinal survey of older Americans that began in 1992. We examined the retirement patterns of a subset of 5,617 HRS respondents who were on a full-time career job at the time of the first interview. Logistic regression was used to explore determinants of re-entry among those who initially exited the labor force. We found that approximately 15 percent of older Americans with career jobs returned to the labor force after initially exiting. Respondents were more likely to re-enter if they were younger, were in better health, or had a defined-contribution pension plan. This research provides empirical evidence of how older Americans are utilizing bridge jobs as they transition from career employment, and that re-entry may be an important part of the work experience of older Americans.

Keywords: Bridge Jobs, Economics of Aging, Partial Retirement, Gradual Retirement JEL No.: J26, J14, J32, H55

I. INTRODUCTION

Retirement for most older Americans with full-time career jobs is not a one-time, permanent event. Labor force exit is more likely to be a process, as more than one half of all career workers take another job before exiting from the labor force completely.[1] The transitional nature of retirement may be even more pronounced if one considers the impact of re-entry among those who exited the labor force directly from their career jobs.[2] Viewed this way, re-entry may be a form of hidden transitional retirement – some individuals who appear to have exited the labor force directly may in fact expect to re-enter, if necessary. Re-entry may therefore remain an option within retirement, further blurring the distinction between work and leisure later in life. This paper examines the prevalence and determinants of re-entry, or "unretirement," and examines the extent to which the possibility of re-entry is part of the initial retirement decision. To what extent is re-entry viewed as a contingency plan in the face of uncertainty in retirement?

Retirement is a period of uncertainty for many reasons. In terms of income security, the fairly recent shift towards a do-it-yourself approach to retirement combined with the current financial crisis is likely to make retirement even more uncertain for many. [3] In particular, the movement away from traditional defined-benefit pensions over the past 20 years has been a key change in the retirement income landscape.[4] Between 1983 and 2004 the percentage of workers with a pension who had a defined-benefit plan decreased from 62 percent to 20 percent, and many of the defined-benefit plans that remained were converted to cash balance plans.[5] Defined-contribution plans, in which workers decide how much to contribute and how to invest their funds, have largely taken the place of defined-benefit plans.[6] Employees with defined-contribution plans assume the investment risk associated with their pension plans. The result is that the pension wealth of many older workers and retirees is now more susceptible to market fluctuations. Further, expected changes to Social Security that will be required to maintain program solvency, such as further increases in the normal retirement age or benefit reductions, are likely to continue the shift towards the do-it-yourself approach.[7]

One way workers can respond to these changes is to remain working later in life. Indeed, older workers are doing this already as a century-old trend towards earlier and earlier retirement among American men halted in the mid-1980s.[8] Labor force participation rates among older men and especially women have increased in recent years.[9] Another way workers can respond is to leave the labor force and adjust consumption to match their retirement income. This approach has the disadvantage of reducing living standards, although retirees may be better off if the reduction in well-being due to lower consumption is offset by the benefits of the additional leisure.

Re-entry can be viewed as a blend of these two approaches -- a way that individuals can leave the labor force in the face of uncertainty with the option of returning later, if necessary. In fact, this option may be part of the retirement decision. If so, an examination of actual work decisions later in life might not provide a complete picture of gradual retirement because a fraction of those who exit the labor force directly from their full-time career job may actually be expecting to return if retirement income falls short of expectations, if retirement is not fulfilling, or for any number of reasons. These "retirees" are actually workers on reserve.

This paper examines the prevalence and determinants of re-entry. Our study is based on data from the Health and Retirement Study (HRS), a nationally-representative survey of various cohorts of older Americans that began in 1992.[10] The cohort of interest in this study is the HRS Core sample, those born between 1931 and 1941. This sample consists of approximately 12,600 individuals from 7,600 households, interviewed every other year from 1992 to 2008.

The next section of the paper provides some relevant background and an overview of the relevant literature on transitional retirement. Section III describes the dataset and methods used in the study, with a detailed description of a key sub-sample used in the analysis – employees who have had a career job in their work history. Section IV presents the findings and Section V summarizes the results of the study.

II. Background

The existing literature on re-entry, or "unretirement," can be separated into two categories: (1) studies that examine re-entry later in life in response to an unexpected event, and (2) studies that consider re-entry in the context of retirement transitions more generally. An example of the former is Chan and Stevens (2001) who investigated re-entry patterns of older workers who had been displaced by layoffs or plant closings. They found that about three quarters of these displaced workers in their 50s re-entered the labor force within two years of job loss, and that reentry rates decreased with age. One important aspect of this paper is that this set of re-entrants included individuals who did not consider themselves retired, but instead as unemployed and looking for work. Another key aspect of the Chan and Stevens research is that they compared workers who had been displaced with those who had not been displaced to show that displacement has a long-term negative effect on subsequent employment probabilities.

A second example of this body of research is Coile and Levine (2006) who investigated re-entry in the context of the booming stock market valuations of the late 1990s and the subsequent bust from 2000 to 2002. Using HRS data and a model of re-entry that controlled for economic and demographic characteristics they found no statistically significant impact of the stock market decline on the rate of re-entry.

Articles that examine re-entry in the context of retirement transitions more generally are more relevant to our study. One early study by Blau (1994) investigated transitions among older workers approaching retirement. Using quarterly data from the Retirement History Survey, Blau found both higher rates of exit and re-entry compared to studies that had utilized annual or biannual data. He found that approximately 26 percent of older men who were not employed transitioned either to part-time or full-time employment, while 23 percent of part-time employed men returned to full-time employment. Blau also found that the quarterly hazard rate for transitioning from out of the labor force to full-time employment was five percent for 56 year olds. This rate remained high until age 62 and then fell below one percent by age 64. The hazard rate of re-entry to part-time employment never rose above 1.2 percent.

A study that is particularly relevant to this paper is Maestas (2007) who examined the extent to which re-entry was anticipated prior to retirement. Utilizing the first six waves of HRS data, Maestas analyzed retirement transitions using self-identified retirement status at different points in time. Maestas found that about one half of workers retired in the "traditional" fashion, directly from either full-time or part-time employment to full retirement (complete labor force withdrawal). Maestas then focused on the transitions that workers made from retirement: from complete retirement to partial retirement (i.e., a self report of "retirement" combined with non- full-time employment), from complete retirement to full-time employment, and from partial retirement to full-time employment. Maestas found that between 16 and 26 percent of retirees returned to the labor force by the sixth wave of the HRS (2002). As expected, she found that unretirement rates were substantially higher among those who first retired in their early to mid 50s than among those who first retired later in life. Maestas established that returns to the labor force can be common among retirees and that labor force participation during retirement was expected, before retirement, by over 80 percent of unretirees. Unretirement was simply a method by which workers could smooth the eventual transition from employment to full retirement.

One caveat with some of the re-entry studies in the literature is the reliance on self-reported retirement, which can be an unreliable measure. Our paper addresses this issue by using actual work status at the time of each survey to identify retirement transitions. Our analysis also uses nine waves of HRS data. This extended time period, from 1992 to 2008, allows for numerous work-leisure combinations over time and reveals a variety of interesting paths to retirement.

III. Data and Methods

The Health and Retirement Study (HRS) is a nationally-representative, longitudinal survey of older Americans that began in 1992.[11] Surveys have taken place every other year since then and we utilize data through 2008. The HRS core respondents were aged 51 to 61 at the time of their first interview in 1992. Each HRS survey contains detailed information on the demographic and economic characteristics of the sample. Key features of the survey for this paper are the questions related to respondents' expectations about retirement and their actual work status in each wave. The original set of HRS respondents included about 12,600 persons from approximately 7,600 households. Attrition from one wave to the next ranged from four to nine percent: after six years (4 waves) about 81 percent of the sample remained, and after 16 years about 62 percent remained.

This paper focuses on labor force exit and retirement patterns, so we excluded respondents with no work experience after age 49. The vast majority of HRS men and women had work experience later in life, as shown in Table 1. Just over 90 percent of men in the sample worked since age 49. Work experience was somewhat lower among women with 78 percent of the sample having work experience after age 49.

Table 1. Sample Size by Gender, Survey Participation, and Work Status.

HRS Core: Respondents Aged 5 1-61 in 1992			
	Men	**Women**	**Total**
Particpated in wave 1			
n	5,869	6,783	12,652
Worked since age 49			
n	5,353	5,286	10,639
% of HRS Core	91%	78%	84%
Had FTC job after age 49			
n	4,288	3,144	7,432
% of HRS Core	73%	46%	59%
On FTC in 1992			
n	3,061	2,556	5,617
% of HRS Core	52%	38%	44%

We made an additional restriction based on whether a respondent, since age 49, had a full- time career (FTC) job, defined as one that consists of 1,600 or more hours per year (i.e., full- time) and that lasted for 10 or more years (i.e., career). The longitudinal nature of the HRS allowed us to do this because the initial questionnaire asked about a respondent's current job and all previous jobs that lasted five years or more. If a respondent was not working at the time of the wave 1 interview, he or she was asked about the most recent job held, regardless of tenure. We found that 73 percent of men and 46 percent of women had a FTC job since age 49.

The bulk of our analysis required that the set of respondents be restricted to those with FTC jobs at the time of their first interview because the first HRS survey contains key questions about retirement expectations and work-related questions. Among the HRS sample, 52 percent of men (n = 3,061) and 38 percent of women (n = 2,556) were on a FTC job in 1992.

IV. Results

The Prevalence of Re-entry

Our analysis begins with a group of HRS respondents who had a full-time career job after age 49. We followed these individuals over time and documented whether and how they left that job and, in some cases, the labor force. Among the HRS respondents for whom we can track employment activity, about 23 percent of men and women were either still on a FTC job in 2008 or were last observed to have been on a FTC job, and another 19 to 21 percent were still on a bridge job in 2008 (Table 2). About one half of the respondents were out of the labor force at the time of the 2008 interview.

The respondents of particular interest in this study are those who were working at the time of or prior to the 2002 interview and who were out of the labor force for at least two consecutive waves following their FTC job.[12] About 8 percent of sample men and women fell into this category. Most of these individuals had initially exited directly from their FTC job, although some were observed to have moved to a bridge job following FTC employment, then were out for at least two waves, and then re-entered.[13]

Demographic and Economic Characteristics of Re-entrants

A key question for this study is how respondents who re-entered the labor force compared to those who remained retired. To answer this question we used detailed information on demographic and economic characteristics that were available at the time the respondents left their FTC jobs. In order to perform the analysis in this way, an additional restriction to the sample was required. Specifically, the analysis was based on respondents who were on a FTC job as of 1992. An advantage of this approach is that we did not rely on information that was provided retrospectively by respondents. The main disadvantage is that the sample size was reduced from 7,432 to 5,617 respondents. Among the sample, 426 (244 men and 182 women) individuals who were on a FTC job in 1992 had exited the labor force for two or more subsequent waves, and then re-entered.

Re-entry was more common among those who were younger and in better health at the time of their transition from the FTC job (Table 3). Approximately three quarters of the men who re-entered were less than age 62 compared to about two thirds of those who remained out. At the other end of the distribution, seven percent of men who re-entered were aged 65 or older at the time of transition compared to 13 percent of those who remained out. About one half of men made a transition from a FTC job between the ages of 56 and 61. A similar pattern was observed among women.

Table 2. Last Observed Status by 2008 among Respondents Who Had a FTC Job after Age 49 by Gender and Survey Participation.

Work status	Men	Women
FTC job	22.6%	23.3%
Bridge job		
Still on bridge job	20.9%	18.7%
Out		
Still out	21.2%	21.1%
Re-entered	**1.9%**	**1.9%**
Direct exit		
Still out	27.0%	29.2%
Re-entered	**6.4%**	**5.9%**
n	4,288	3,144

Source: Authors' calculations based on the Health and Retirement Study.

Note: Work status could not be determined for 8.1 percent of men and 5.6 percent of women.

Regarding health status, more than one half of all respondents on FTC jobs in 1992 who were out of the labor force for two or more waves rated their health as excellent or very good prior to leaving their FTC job. Among men, 62 percent of those who re-entered rated their health as excellent or very good compared to one half of those who stayed out of the labor force. Those men who re-entered were also less likely than those who remained out to report their health as being fair or poor (11 percent versus 17 percent). Again, a similar pattern was observed among women. This may be indicative of healthy men and women having more opportunity to join the labor market after being out of the labor force for at least two surveys. Good health may result in broader choices of occupations and industries for re-entrants.

With respect to other demographic characteristics, compared to those who remained retired, re-entrants were slightly more likely to have a college degree and were significantly more likely to have dependent children (women only). Spouse's health status did not differ significantly by re-entry status. Spouse's employment status had an impact among both men and women, where those who re-entered were more likely than those who remained out to have an employed spouse, though differences were not statistically significant.

Table 3. Demographic Characteristics Prior to Initial Transition, by Re-entry Status Sample: Respondents With a FTC Job in 1992 and Who Exited by 2008.

Work status	Men		Women	
	Still out	Re-entered	Still out	Re-entered
Age prior to transition**,##,^^				
< 55	17	25	27	42
56 - 61	49	52	49	47
62 - 64	21	17	17	10
65+	13	7	7	2
Subjective Health Status**,##				
excellent or very good	50	62	51	61
good	33	26	33	30
fair or poor	17	11	17	9
College Degree	21	23	21	23
Less than College Degree	79	77	79	77
Married^^	89	91	70	69
Not Married	11	9	30	31
Dependent Children##, ^^	15	17	26	36
No Dependent Children	85	83	74	64
Spouse's Health Status				
excellent or very good	55	57	50	48
good	27	26	32	35
fair or poor	18	17	19	17
Spouse Employed	45	50	39	44
Spouse Not Employed	55	50	61	56
n	1,315	244	1,129	182

*, ** Difference by re-entry status among men is statistically significant at the 5% and 1% level, respectively.

#, ## Difference by re-entry status among women is statistically significant at the 5% and 1% level, respectively.

^, ^^ Difference by gender among those who re-entered is statistically significant at the 5% and 1% level, respectively.

Source: Authors' calculations based on the Health and Retirement Study.

In addition to demographic characteristics, economic factors, including the characteristics of an individual's FTC job, differed by re-entry status. Some key differences are discussed here, while a more exhaustive list is shown in Table 4. Over 37 percent of men who re-entered had defined-benefit pensions on their FTC job while only 24 percent had defined-contribution pensions. The corresponding percentages for those men who remained out of the labor force were 42 and 22 percent. Thus the prevalence of defined-benefit pensions was substantially higher among those who left a FTC job and remained out of the labor force. This relationship was even more evident among women. This difference is consistent with some recent literature on bridge jobs that has found those with defined-benefit plans were less likely to experience a gradual retirement.[14] It is also consistent with the idea that those with defined-benefit plans have a more stable retirement financially and may be less likely to rely on re-entry to supplement their retirement income. Further, this evidence is consistent with the notion that individuals with defined-contribution plans may be more vulnerable in retirement because of investment risk and may be more likely to re-enter after an initial exit.

Individuals who re-entered were also more likely than those who remained out to have had lower wages on the FTC job and lower levels of wealth (men only) at the time of transition, though differences were not statistically significant.[15] About 36 percent of the men and 40 percent of the women who re-entered had been earning less than $10 per hour (1992 dollars) on their FTC job just prior to transition; corresponding percentages for those who remained out of the labor force were approximately five percentage points lower.

A similar story holds with respect to wealth at the time of the transition from FTC employment. Approximately 36 percent of the men who re-entered had less than $25,000 in assets at the time they left their FTC job, compared to about 32 percent among those who remained out. Men who re-entered were also less likely than those who remained out to own a home, 73 percent versus 80 percent among men; there was no difference in home ownership by re-entry status among the women. The issue of wealth prior to retirement is a potential concern for both groups who left the labor force following full-time career employment. Overall, well more than one half of all those who exited had less than $100,000 in assets prior to leaving their FTC job. This may have policy implications if the shift towards a do-it-yourself approach to retirement continues.

Table 4. Economic Characteristics Prior to Initial Transition, by Re-entry Status Sample: HRS Core Respondents with a FTC Job in 1992 and Who Exited by 2008.

Work status	Men		Women	
	Still out	Re-entered	Still out	Re-entered
Health Insurance Status				
Not covered on career job	6	5	7	7
"Covered and would maintain" coverage	80	81	74	80
"Covered and would lose" coverage	14	14	18	14
Pension Status				
No Pension	30	29	29	31
Defined - Contribution only	22	24	26	33
Defined - Benefit only	42	37	41	33
Both DB and DC	6	10	5	4
Self-Employed ##	12	14	6	12
Wage and Salary	88	86	94	88
Occupation Status^^				
White collar, highly skilled	34	35	33	35
White collar, other	13	13	37	34
Blue collar, highly skilled	27	31	8	9
Blue collar, other	26	22	21	22
Wage Rate^^				
$0 - $10/hour	30	36	35	40
$10 - $20/hour	26	23	39	37
$20 - $50/hour	41	38	24	22
> $50/hour	3	4	2	2
Wealth				
$0-$25k	32	36	40	38
$25k-$100k	25	25	22	29
$100k-$500k	33	28	29	27
>$500k	9	11	8	6
Do not own home*	20	27	20	20
Own home	80	73	80	80
n	1,315	244	1,129	182

*, ** Difference by re-entry status among men is statistically significant at the 5% and 1% level, respectively.

#, ## Difference by re-entry status among women is statistically significant at the 5% and 1% level, respectively.

^, ^^ Difference by gender among those who re-entered is statistically significant at the 5% and 1% level, respectively

Source: Authors' calculations based on the Health and Retirement Study.

Given the flexibility associated with self employment, a priori, it seemed that respondents who were self employed on their FTC job would be more likely to re-enter following an exit. The relationship is not as strong as we had expected, however. Among the men, approximately 14 percent of those who re-entered were self employed compared to 12 percent of those who did not re-enter. Among women, the difference was larger and statistically significant, 12 percent versus 6 percent. One possible explanation is that the self employed may be more likely to retire gradually, in stages, while on their career job (an option open to few wage-and-salary workers) rather than leave and then return. Another possibility is that other factors besides self employment are not being held constant, and that these factors are blurring the impact of self employment. To address this issue, we turn to a multivariate approach to examine re-entry.

Determinants of Re-entry

We model the re-entry decision later in life using logistic regression. The sample included individuals who were on a FTC job at the time of the first interview and who were not working for at least two consecutive waves following the FTC job. The dependent variable was equal to one if an individual re-entered the labor force after being out for at least two waves and was equal to zero otherwise. The set of right-hand side variables included the demographic and economic characteristics described above, in addition to other controls such as region and ethnicity. All time-varying variables, such as age, health status, and spouse's employment status, were measured as of the time of the transition from the FTC job. The model was estimated for men and women separately. Selected marginal effects from the regressions, evaluated at sample means, are reported in Table 5.

One of the strongest predictors of re-entry was age, as might be expected. Respondents who were older at the time they left their FTC job were less likely to re-enter the labor force. Men and women who were aged 56 to 61 at the time of transition, for example, were five percentage points less likely to re-enter than those less than age 56; men and women who were aged 62 to 64 were between 8 and 11 percentage points less likely to re-enter than those younger than age 56, and those aged 65 and older were 14 and 23 percentage points less likely to re-enter than those younger than age 56. Respondents who rated their health as fair or poor were less likely to re-enter than those who rated their health as good, although the impact was only marginally significant among men.

Pension status, home ownership, and spousal work status were also significant determinants of re-entry among the men. Men with defined-contribution plans were about 5 percentage points more likely to re-enter relative to those without a pension. This result supports the findings regarding pension status that were found in the descriptive analysis. One difference between men and women in the descriptive analysis was the impact of having a working spouse – men with a working spouse were more likely to re-enter than those without a working spouse, whereas there appeared to be no difference among the women. This result remained in the multivariate analysis. Men with a working spouse were 5 percentage points more likely to reenter than those whose spouses did not work, and the result was significant at the 5 percent level. Women with a working spouse were neither more nor less likely to re-enter than those whose spouse did not work. Regarding home ownership, men who owned a home were 5 percentage points less likely to re-enter, suggesting that home ownership was a sign of financial stability in retirement. Finally, self-employment status was significant only among the women, a finding that is also consistent with the descriptive results.

V. Conclusion

This paper examined the extent to which re-entry plays a role in the retirement process. According to data from the Health and Retirement Study from 1992 to 2008, about 15 percent of the sample of older Americans with full-time career jobs returned to the labor force after exiting and remaining out at least 2 years. Respondents were more likely to re-enter after leaving a FTC job if they were younger, in better health, had a college degree, and had dependent children at the time of the transition (women only). Individuals with employer-provided pensions on the FTC job were also more likely to re-enter than those without pensions. Notably, among the men, being self employed on the FTC job did not have a strong impact the probability of re-entry after an exit. Finally, respondents with lower wages and respondents who did not own a home were more likely to re-enter, though these differences were only marginally significant.

This research provides additional evidence that retirement transitions are even more varied than what is reported in the bridge job literature. Among those who exited the labor force directly from career employment, retirement is often not a one-time, permanent event. A sizable portion of these respondents returned to the labor force. As a result, when bridge job prevalence and re-entry are both taken into account, it is clear that the large majority of older Americans with FTC jobs do not experience a direct exit from the labor force.

Table 5. Selected Marginal Effects from Logistic Regression Dependent Variable: Re-entered by Time t (Re-entered = 1) Sample: HRS Core Respondents With a FTC Job in 1992 and Who Exited the Labor Force by 2008.

	Men		Women	
	coefficient	**p-value**	**coefficient**	**p-value**
Age				
56 or younger				
56-61	-0.053 **	0.019	-0.055**	0.004
62-64	-0.078**	0.005	-0.105**	0.001
65 or older	-0.142**	0.000	-0.230**	0.000
Respondent Health				
Excellent/very good	0.033	0.107	0.030	0.124
Good				
Fair/poor	-0.042	0.196	-0.077**	0.018
Pension Status				
Defined-benefit	0.011	0.629	-0.010	0.642
Defined-contribution	0.048**	0.034	0.035	0.119
Both	0.021	0.630	-0.038	0.533
None				
Self Employed	0.040	0.227	0.071**	0.024
Spouse works	0.046**	0.036	0.039	0.149
Own Home	-0.045*	0.068	0.018	0.47 1
Constant	-0.117**	0.000	-0.144**	0.000
Female				

Source: Authors' calculations based on the Health and Retirement Study.

REFERENCES

[1] Blau, D. M. (1994). Labor Force Dynamics of Older Men. *Econometrica*, Vol. *62*, No. 1, pp. 117-156.

[2] Cahill, K. E., Giandrea, M. D. & Quinn, J. F. (2006). Retirement Patterns from Career Employment. *The Gerontologist, 46*(4), 514-523.

[3] Cahill, K. E. & Soto, M. (2003). How Do Cash Balance Plans Affect the Pension Landscape? Issue in Brief 14 (December). Chestnut Hill, MA: Center for Retirement Research at Boston College.

[4] Chan, S. & Stevens A. H. (2001). Job Loss and Employment Patterns of Older Workers. *Journal of Labor Economics*, Vol. *19*, No. 2, pp. 484-521.

[5] Coile, C. C. & Levine, P. B. (2006). Bulls, Bears, and Retirement

Behavior. *Industrial and Labor Relations Review*, Vol. *59*, No. 3, pp. 408-429.

[6] Eschtruth, A. D. & Gemus, J. (2002). Are Older Workers Responding to the Bear Market? *Just the Facts on Retirement Issues*, No. *5* (September). Chestnut Hill, MA: Center for Retirement Research at Boston College.

[7] Giandrea, M. D., Cahill, K. E. & Quinn, J. F. (2009). Bridge Jobs: A Comparison Across Cohorts. *Research on Aging*, Vol. *31*, No. 5, pp. 549-576.

[8] Juster, F. T. & Suzman, R. (1995). An Overview of the Health and Retirement Study. *Journal of Human Resources* , *30*(Supplement), S7-S56.

[9] Maestas, N. (2007). Back to Work: Expectations and Realizations of Work after Retirement. Rand Working Paper WR-196-2.

[10] Munnell, A. H. (2003). The Declining Role of Social Security. Just the Facts: On Retirement Issues, No. 6. (February) Chestnut Hill, MA: Center for Retirement Research at Boston College.

[11] Munnell, A. H., Cahill, K. E., Eschtruth, A. D. & and Sass, S. A. (2004). The Graying of Massachusetts: Aging, the New Rules of Retirement, and the Changing Workforce. The Massachusetts Institute for a New Commonwealth (MassINC).

[12] Munnell, A. H. & Perun, P. (2006). An Update on Private Pensions. Issue in Brief 50 (August). Chestnut Hill, MA: Center for Retirement Research at Boston College.

[13] Munnell, A. H. & Sundén, A. (2004). *Coming Up Short: The Challenge of 401(k) Plans*. The Brookings Institution Press.

[14] Mutchler, J. E., Burr, J. A., Pienta, A. M. & Massagli, M. P. (1997). Pathways to Labor Force Exit: Work transitions and work instability. *Journal of Gerontology: Social Sciences*, *52B(1)*, S4-S12.

[15] Purcell, P. J. (2007). Older Workers: Employment and Retirement Trends. CRS Report for Congress, Congressional Research Service. The Library of Congress. Washington, DC.

[16] Quinn, J. F. (1999). Retirement Patterns and Bridge Jobs in the 1990s. EBRI Issue Brief, No. 206 (February). Washington, DC: Employee Benefit Research Institute. 1-23.

[17] Quinn, J. F. (2000). New Paths to Retirement. In *Forecasting Retirement Needs and Retirement Wealth* (Brett Hammond, Olivia Mitchell, and Anna Rappaport, editors). Philadelphia, PA: University of Pennsylvania Press: 13-32.

[18] Reimers, C. & Honig, H. (1996). Responses to Social Security by Men and Women: Myopic and Far-Sighted Behavior. *The Journal of Human Resources*, Vol. *31*, No. 2 (Spring, 1996), pp. 359-382.

[19] The Board of Trustees, Federal Old-Age and Survivors Insurance and Federal Disability Insurance Trust Funds (2007). *The 2007 Annual Report of the Board of Trustees of the Federal Old-Age and Survivors Insurance and Federal Disability Insurance Trust Funds*. U.S. Government Printing Office. Washington, D.C.

End Notes

[1] Mutchler et al. (1997); Quinn (1999, 2000); Cahill, Giandrea, and Quinn (2006); Giandrea, Cahill, and Quinn (2008).

[2] Maestas (2007).

[3] Munnell, et al. (2004).

[4] Munnell and Sundén (2004).

[5] Munnell and Perun (2006). Cahill and Soto (2003) provide more information on cash balance plans which are often referred to as "hybrid" pension plans, because they contain characteristics of both defined-benefit and defined- contribution plans.

[6] Munnell and Sundén (2004).

[7] Munnell (2003); The Board of Trustees, Federal Old-Age and Survivors Insurance and Federal Disability Insurance Trust Funds (2007).

[8] Quinn (1999).

[9] Eschtruth and Gemus (2002); Purcell (2007).

[10] Juster and Suzman (1995).

[11] Juster and Suzman (1995).

[12] We require respondents to be out of the labor force for at least two surveys in order to avoid misclassifying respondents who had a temporary lull in employment only. Therefore, respondents had to exit the labor force by the time of the 2002 interview in order to qualify for re-entry status (e.g., worked in 2002; out in 2004 and 2006; reentered in 2008). While this re-entry criterion requires a respondent to be out of the labor force for at least two interviews, re-entry could in fact occur after a much longer period.

[13] We were unable to identify retirement transitions for about 8 percent of the sample. These individuals are not considered in the percentages calculated above.

[14] See Cahill, Giandrea, and Quinn (2006).

[15] Wealth does not include the value of the primary residence or of any defined-benefit pension plans vested in the worker.

In: Older Workers Navigating Employment and... ISBN: 978-1-61470-253-5
Editors: Benjamin V. Chase

Chapter 4

SELF-EMPLOYMENT TRANSITIONS AMONG OLDER AMERICAN WORKERS WITH CAREER JOBS

U.S. Bureau of Labor Statistics

ABSTRACT

What role does self-employment play in the retirement process? Older Americans are staying in the labor force longer than prior trends would have predicted and many change jobs later in life. These job transitions are often within the same occupation or across occupations within wage-and-salary employment. The transition can also be out of wage-and-salary work and into self employment. Indeed, national statistics show that self employment becomes more prevalent with age, partly because self employment provides older workers with opportunities not found in traditional wage-and-salary jobs, such as flexibility in hours worked and independence. This paper analyzes transitions into and out of self employment among older workers who have had career jobs. We utilize the Health and Retirement Study, a nationally-representative dataset of older Americans, to investigate the prevalence of self employment among older workers who made a job transition later in life and to explore the factors that determine the choice of wageand-salary employment or self employment. We find that post-career transitions into and out of self employment are common and that health status, career occupation, and financial variables are important determinants of these transitions. As older Americans and the country as a whole face financial strains in retirement income in the years ahead, self employment may be a vital part of the pro-work solution.

I. INTRODUCTION

Older Americans are staying in the labor force longer than prior trends would have predicted and they often change jobs later in life.[1] In fact, the majority of older Americans who have had career jobs make a job transition prior to retirement.[2] These transitions are often within the same occupation or across occupations within wage-and-salary employment. The transition can also be out of wage-and-salary work and into self employment. National statistics show that self employment becomes more prevalent with age,[3] partly because self employment provides older workers with opportunities not found in traditional wage-and-salary jobs, such as hours flexibility and independence. This paper examines the prevalence and determinants of a specific type of self-employment transition – those that serve as a step in the retirement process.

Self-employment transitions prior to retirement are of particular importance to policymakers and employers. The leading edge of the Baby Boomers have now reached retirement age, and their movement out of the labor force is expected to strain existing sources of retirement income. Today, the ratio of workers to retirees is about three to one; by 2030, the ratio will be two to one.[4] As fewer workers support a growing retiree population, policymakers may look for ways to encourage individuals to remain in the labor force.

Self employment may be one option because self-employed individuals tend to stay in the labor force longer than wage-and-salary workers. While some of the differences between self- employed workers and wage-and-salary employees may be explained by selection effects (i.e., those who choose self employment are those who would have worked later in life anyway), self employment offers real advantages that are valued by older workers such as working for oneself and flexible work hours.[5] Older workers may also have access to capital that makes a transition to self employment possible and they have a lifetime of experience to increase the probability of a successful business venture. To the extent that self employment keeps individuals in the labor force longer than they otherwise would have, the country as a whole benefits from their additional output. These workers remain productive, have higher incomes, and will be less dependent on public programs, all as the nation has more goods and services to distribute among an aging population.

Employers may also have a lot to learn from these transitions, especially as older workers become an increasingly attractive option to fill an expected shortfall in skilled workers. Workers who switch from wage-and-salary employment to self employment later in life may be opting for self employment because of what is lacking in wage-and-salary employment rather than what can be gained in self employment. Workers' choices indicate that many select self employment and the benefits derived from it even when facing considerable risk in the form of returns to capital and variation in expected earnings. Employers may be able to woo those workers back to wage-and-salary employment – or prevent the transitions to begin with – by offering older workers some of the advantages that currently may be found predominantly in self employment. Flexibility in work schedule is a classic example.

This paper analyzes transitions into and out of self employment among older workers who have had career jobs. The next section of the paper provides some background on the role of self employment in the retirement transitions of older workers. Section III describes the data set that we utilize for the analysis, the Health and Retirement Study, an ongoing longitudinal survey of 12,652 older Americans that began in 1992. Section IV presents the results of our analysis and Section V summarizes the main points of the paper.

II. Background

A dominant theme in the self-employment literature is the role of financial capital in entrepreneurship. This section highlights a few key studies that address this theme, and several studies related to self-employment transitions later in life. Perhaps one of the most informative studies on self employment is by Evans and Jovanovic (1989), who developed a model of self- employment based, in part, on the role of liquidity constraints. In this model, a person becomes self employed if expected income from wage-and-salary employment does not exceed income from self employment. Using a sample of young men in the National Longitudinal Survey of Youth, Evans and Jovanovic found that the value of assets had a positive effect on the likelihood of becoming self employed. Moreover, they found a positive correlation between assets and self- employment income, which may imply that men with greater assets become more profitable entrepreneurs.

Holtz-Eakin, Joulfaian, and Rosen (1994a) developed a related model of self employment where the decision to become an entrepreneur was dependent on assets and personal characteristics. They found that an inheritance has a positive effect on the probability of becoming self employed, other things equal, but that the impact of an inheritance decreased with wealth. This finding confirmed the results presented in Evans and Jovanovic (1989). In another article Holtz-Eakin, Joulfaian, and Rosen (1994b) found that the receipt of an inheritance while self employed increased the viability and revenues of the self-employed worker's business.

Dunn and Holtz-Eakin (2000) investigated not only the relationship between financial capital and entrepreneurship, but also the impact of human capital on self-employment decisions. They estimated a model that included own and family assets, demographic variables, and parents' self-employment status. Own assets had a positive but small effect on the likelihood of becoming self-employed, while parents' self-employment experience exerted a large and positive impact on the probability of becoming self employed.

Several studies have focused on self employment among older workers. Fuchs (1982) considered the role of self employment among older workers by focusing on the transitions from wage-and-salary employment to self employment. He found that the self employed were significantly more likely to continue to work, particularly by reducing work hours. Other factors that impacted the employment decision of older workers included health, age, and pension eligibility. One interesting finding was that the probability of switching from wage-and-salary employment to self employment was a function of a worker's occupational experience in jobs that required skills similar to those needed in self employment. Examples included managerial and sales positions.

Bruce, Holtz-Eakin, and Quinn (2000) focused on older workers and the transitions among wage-and-salary employment, self employment, and labor force non-participation using the first three waves of Health and Retirement Study data. They found that liquidity constraints played an important role in determining who became self employed. Moreover, they concluded that health insurance was not an important factor affecting the transition from wage-and-salary to self employment.

Hipple (2004) documented that self employment became more likely as workers age. The incidence of unincorporated self employment in 2003 by age bracket was 7.4 percent for those age 35 to 44, 8.2 percent for those age 45 to 54, 10.5 percent for those age 55 to 64, and 15.3 percent for those 65 and older. Most recently, Zissimopoulos, Maestas, and Karoly (2007) examined determinants of labor force exit among wage-and-salary and self-employed older workers, and found that defined benefit pension incentives were significant determinants of why exit rates were higher among wage and salary workers. Further, using a cross-country comparison of the United States and Britain, they found that the availability of publicly-provided health insurance impacted labor force exit.

This paper contributes to the literature by focusing on transitions later in life from wageand-salary career jobs into self employment and from self-employed career jobs into wage-andsalary employment. One explanation for the shift to self employment later in life may be a change in preferences for leisure as individuals age and leave full-time career (FTC) employment. The mechanics behind this explanation can be seen graphically in Figure 1, in which the choice between wage-and-salary and self employment is simplified by focusing on the tradeoff between higher wages and hours flexibility (i.e., wage-and-salary workers have higher earnings relative to self employed workers, but they are constrained in their ability to reduce hours worked). The hours inflexibility associated with wage-and-salary employment is illustrated by the vertical line at point L, the maximum amount of leisure allowed under wageand-salary employment. In the first case, a worker chooses the higher wages and lower leisure hours associated with wage-and-salary employment. In the second case, perhaps one that follows FTC employment, the worker sacrifices higher wages in return for the increased leisure available with self employment.

Case I: Worker prefers wage-and-salary employment

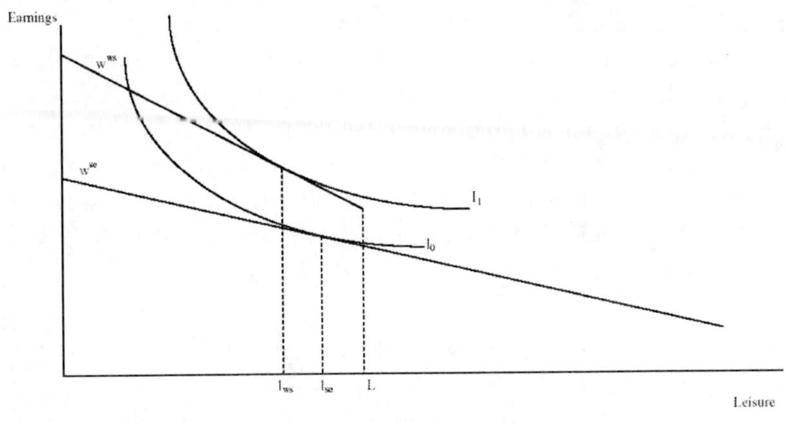

Figure 1. (Continued).

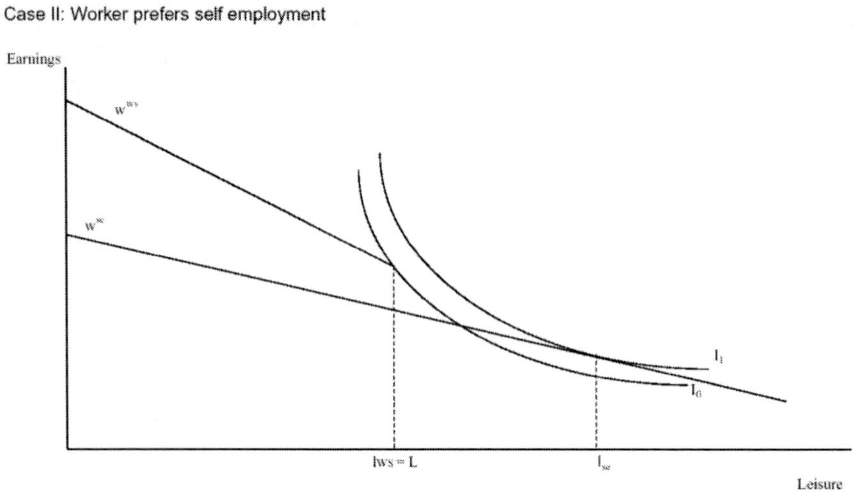

Figure 1. The Choice between Wage-and-Salary Work and Self Employment.

The underlying assumption about hours inflexibility in wage-and-salary employment is supported by several stylized facts. In some cases, high fixed costs per worker related to benefits such as health insurance limit a firm's willingness to employ part-time workers. In other cases, defined-benefit pension rules may result in significantly smaller pension valuations for those who work part-time (Penner, Perun, and Steuerle, 2002; Burkhauser and Quinn, 1997). While self employed workers may not experience these constraints on hours worked, they instead typically face lower wage profiles than comparable full-time wage-and-salary workers. Hamilton (2000) found a 35 percent earnings differential in favor of wage-and-salary workers relative to self-employed workers, and Lettau (1994) found that part-time workers earn substantially less in part-time work than in equivalent full-time work.

Using this simplified framework and the existing literature on self employment as a guide, we extend the research on retirement transitions more generally by Cahill, Giandrea and Quinn (2006) to incorporate switches later in life from wage-and-salary employment to self- employment and vice versa.

III. Data

An ideal data set for this research is the Health and Retirement Study (HRS). The HRS is a nationally representative panel data set created with the objective of understanding the antecedents and consequences of retirement, monitoring work disability, and examining the relationship among health, income and wealth, and the patterns of wealth accumulation and consumption over time.[6] The HRS survey began in 1992 with interviews of over 12,500 people (known as the Core) aged 51 to 61 years, and their spouses, whatever their age. The interviews have been repeated every other year since 1992.

The longitudinal nature of the HRS allows us to examine each respondent's work history and identify job transitions. For the purposes of this analysis, we define a full-time career job as one that consists of at least 1,600 hours per year ("full time") and that lasts ten or more years ("career"). Jobs that follow FTC jobs and precede labor force withdrawal are considered bridge jobs. These definitions are consistent with earlier studies investigating bridge job behavior.

We begin our analysis by focusing on individuals who have had work experience since age 49, and obtain a sample of 10,540 HRS respondents (Table 1). We find that 91 percent of age-eligible men (n=5,344) and 77 percent of age-eligible women (n=5,196) have worked since age 50. Because this paper focuses on transitions from career employment, we restrict the sample to respondents with a FTC job at the time of the first interview, which reduces the sample to 5,570 respondents. Slightly more than one half of the men (n=3,057) and one third of the women (n=2,513) were on a FTC job in 1992. Approximately 21 percent of the men and 10 percent of the women were self employed on their FTC jobs at the time of the first interview. Therefore, among those HRS respondents who were on a FTC job at the time of the first interview, 4,668 were wage-and-salary workers and 902 were self-employed.

IV. RESULTS

Descriptive Statistics: Outcomes

We begin the descriptive analysis with a high-level overview of how the prevalence of self employment increases as FTC workers age. Figure 2 presents the percentage of HRS men and women on FTC jobs in 1992 who were working for pay in each interview, from 1992 to 2004. By 2004, fewer than half of respondents, now aged 63 to 73, were working. Women were somewhat more likely to be working than men, a result of the fact that women were younger, on average, at the time of the first interview and the fact that FTC status was a requirement to be included in the analysis.

Table 1. Sample Size, by Gender HRS Core: Respondents Age 51 to 61 in 1992.

	Men	Women	Total
All HRS Core respondents			
n	5,869	6,783	12,652
Worked since age 50			
n	5,344	5,196	10,540
% of HRS Core	91%	77%	83%
Worked since age 50 and had a FTC job			
n	4,697	3,470	8,167
% of HRS Core	80%	51%	65%
On a FTC job in 1992			
n	3,057	2,513	5,570
% of HRS Core	52%	37%	44%
Wage and salary			
n	2,418	2,250	4,668
% of FTC in 1992	79%	90%	84%
Self employed			
n	639	263	902
% of FTC in 1992	21%	10%	16%

Source: Authors' calculations based on data from the Health and Retirement Study.

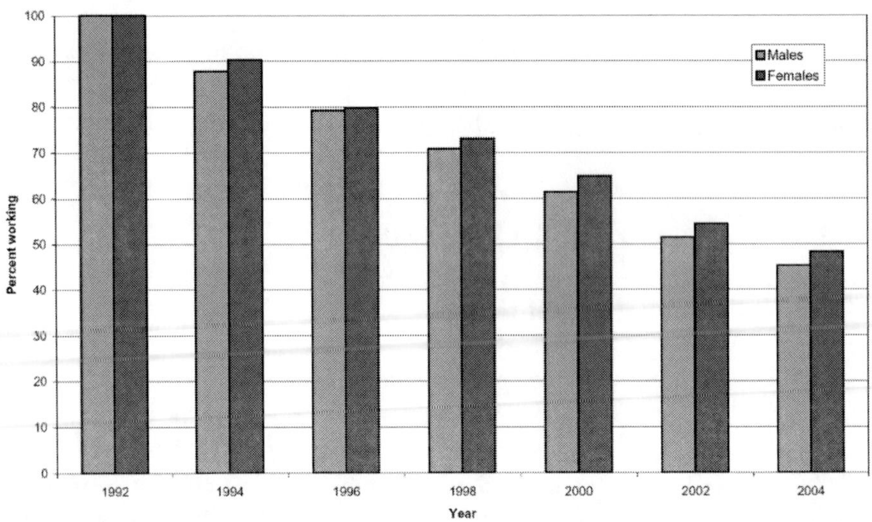

Figure 2. Percent Working, by Gender, 1992 – 2004 Sample: HRS Core Respondents On a FTC Job in 1992.

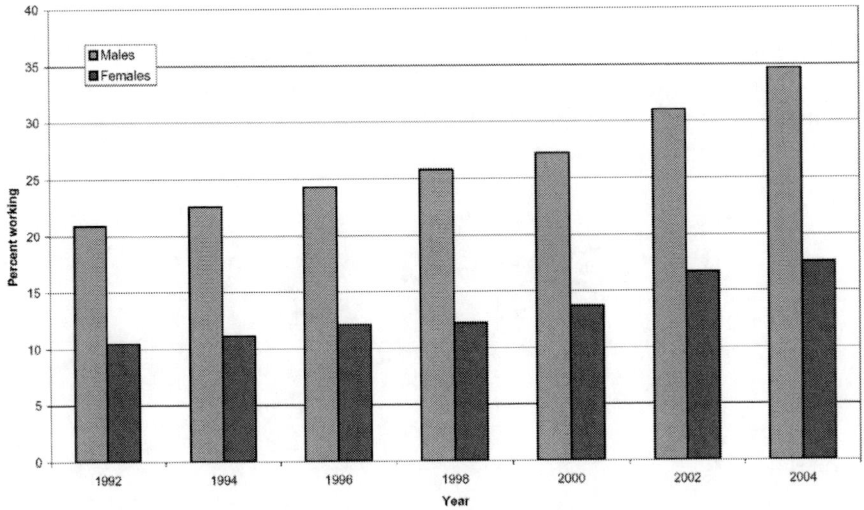

Figure 3. Percent Self Employed among those Working, by Gender, 1992 – 2004
Sample: HRS Core Respondents On a FTC Job in 1992.

As the FTC respondents exited the labor force, the percentage of those working who were self employed increased substantially (Figure 3). At the time of the 1992 survey, slightly more than 20 percent of the men were self employed. The percentage of respondents who were self employed among those who remained working rose in every survey year through 2004, with the largest increases in the 2002 and 2004 surveys. Between 2000 and 2004, the percentage of men who were self employed among those who had a FTC job in 1992 and who were still working in 2004 increased more than 7 percentage points to nearly 35 percent. A similar pattern was seen among the women, although the percentages were considerably lower. Among women with FTC jobs in 1992 and still working in 2004, about 17 percent were self employed on their 2004 job.

The rise in self employment as workers age is a function of two factors. First, self employed workers may transition out of the labor force more slowly than wage-and-salary workers. Second, more wage-and-salary workers could be shifting into self employment as they grow older than vice versa. The longitudinal nature of the HRS allows us to examine both of these mechanisms separately. Rates of transition out of the labor force by self-employment and wage-and-salary status among men with FTC jobs are shown in Figure 4a. Those who were self employed on their FTC job in 1992 exited the labor force more gradually than those on wageand-salary jobs. In particular, about one third of men who were self employed in 1992 were no longer working by 2004, compared to about 60 percent of the wage-and-salary men. A difference also exists among the female sample (Figure 4b), although the 10 percentage point gap between self-employed and wage-and-salary women in 2004 was not quite as large as among men.

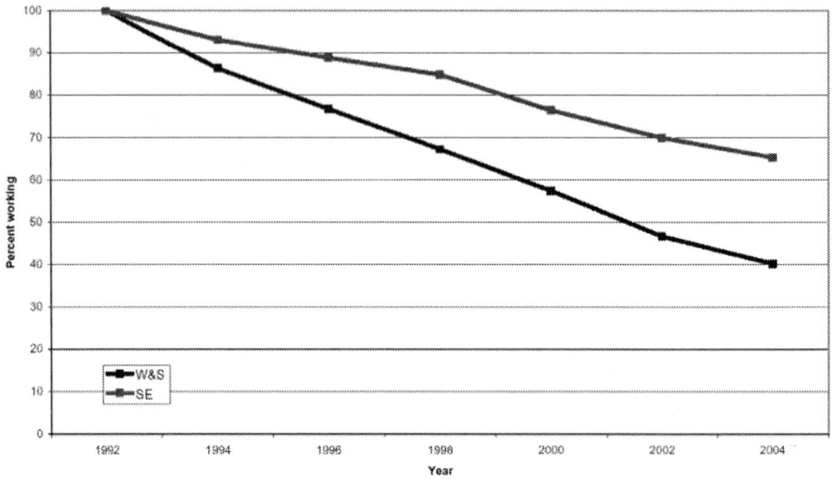

Figure 4a. Percent Working, by Self Employment Status in 1992, 1992 – 2004 Sample: HRS Core Males On a FTC Job in 1992.

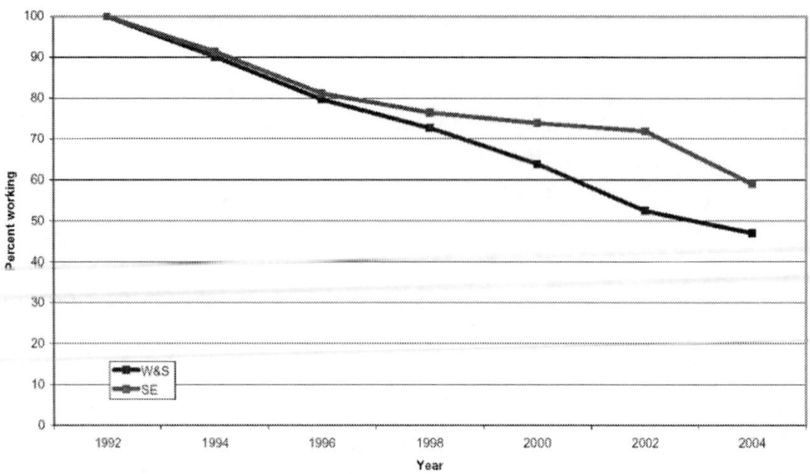

Figure 4b. Percent Working, by Self Employment Status in 1992, 1992 – 2004 Sample: HRS Core Females On a FTC Job in 1992.

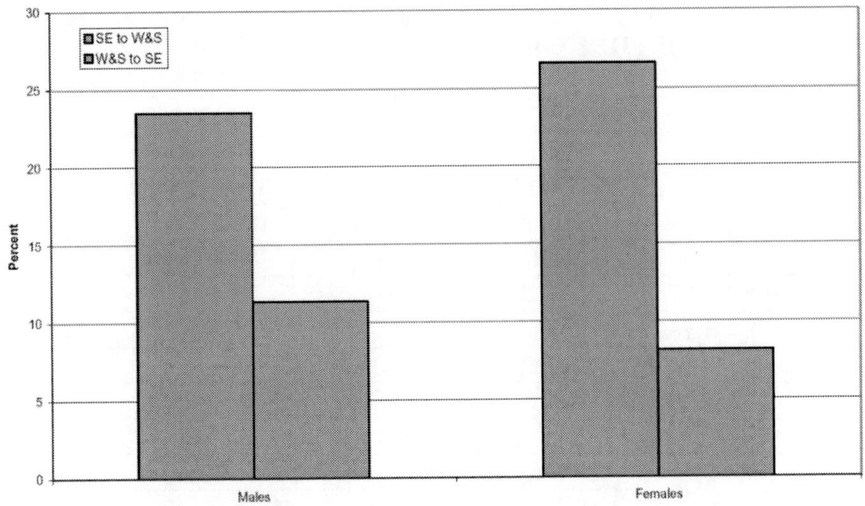

Figure 5. Percent of Individuals Who Switched Work Status between 1992 and 2004, by Gender Sample: HRS Respondents On a FTC Job in 1992.

The second explanation for the observed increase in self employment as workers age is that more wage-and-salary workers shift into self employment than self-employed workers shift into wage-and-salary employment. In percentage terms, men who were self employed on their FTC job moved into wage-and-salary worked at a much higher rate (about 23 percent) than wage-and-salary men moved into self employment (about 11 percent) (Figure 5). But because there were so many more wage-and-salary workers relative to self-employed workers, about 4 to 1, the net impact was a rise in self employment. Again, a similar story held among women.

Before proceeding with an analysis of determinants, it is important to highlight a key distinction between the self-employed and wage-and-salary jobs noted above; namely, that those on self employed jobs are much more likely to be working part time (Table 2). Among men who were on a wage-and-salary FTC job in 1992 and who were still working in 2002, about three quarters were working full time in 2002. In contrast, only about 56 percent of their self- employed counterparts were working full time in 2002. Among women, the gap was even wider. So it is important to note that while self-employed workers were staying in the workforce later in life, the hours worked does not appear to match those among wage-and-salary workers, at least with respect to a full-time, part-time distinction.

Table 2. Self Employment Status by Full-time/Part-time Status, Year and Gender Sample: HRS Core Respondents on a FTC Job in 1992 Men.

Men					
	n	Wage & Salary		Self Employed	
		Full Time	Part Time	Full Time	Part Time
1992	3,057	100%	0%	100%	0%
1994	2,427	96%	4%	86%	14%
1996	2,078	91%	9%	73%	27%
1998	1,782	86%	14%	65%	35%
2000	1,447	80%	20%	61%	39%
2002	1,180	72%	28%	56%	44%
Women					
	n	Wage & Salary		Self Employed	
		Full Time	Part Time	Full Time	Part Time
1992	2,513	100%	0%	100%	0%
1994	2,110	92%	8%	85%	15%
1996	1,771	88%	12%	65%	35%
1998	1,568	84%	16%	70%	30%
2000	1,331	77%	23%	63%	37%
2002	1,103	72%	28%	51%	49%

Source: Authors' calculations based on data from the Health and Retirement Study.

Table 3. Transitions Into and From Self Employment as of 2004 Sample: HRS Core Respondents on FTC Jobs in Wave One.

	Still on a FTC Job	Moved to Self Employment	Moved to Wage and Salary	Out	SE (SE+WS −Out)	WS (SE+WS +Out)
Wage and salary						
Males	10.6%	10.4%	31.7%	47.3%	11.6%	
Females	17.0	7.9	36.2	38.9	9.5	
Self employment						
Males	23.1	23.3	32.0	21.6		41.6%
Females	17.1	26.9	32.1	23.9		38.7

Source: Authors' calculations based on data from the Health and Retirement Study.

Table 4a. Transitions Into Self Employment as of 2004, by Demographic Characteristics Sample: HRS Core Respondents on Wage and Salary FTC Jobs in Wave One.

Determinants	Men						Women					
	Category Percentage	Still on a FTC Job	Moved to Self Employment	Moved to Wage & Salary	Out	SE (SE+WS+Out)	Category Percentage	Still on a FTC Job	Moved to Self Employment	Moved to Wage & Salary	Out	SE (SE+WS+Out)
Age in 2004												
61 and younger	4.4%	34.2%	6.6%	34.2%	25.0%	10.0%	27.8%	41.1%	8.5%	31.8%	18.7%	14.5%
62 - 64	30.2	21.9	10.8	36.9	30.4	13.8	26.4	22.1	9.8	38.2	29.9	12.6
65 - 69	42.1	10.3	11.3	30.9	47.5	12.6	33.5	10.4	6.8	37.9	45.0	7.5
70 and older	23.3	3.7	13.0	29.9	53.4	13.5	12.3	3.6	8.5	26.9	61.0	8.8
Subjective health status												
excellent/ very good	60.1	14.7	13.0	32.3	40.1	15.2	62.4	24.2	9.5	35.8	30.5	12.6
good	29.8	12.3	10.5	33.3	44.0	12.0	28.5	17.4	6.6	34.1	41.9	8.0
fair/poor	10.1	8.6	4.0	32.8	54.6	4.4	9.1	12.1	4.9	31.5	51.5	5.5
Less than college degree	76.2	12.0	9.1	33.9	44.9	10.4	78.3	20.6	7.4	34.7	37.4	9.3
College degree	23.8	17.6	18.3	28.5	35.6	22.2	21.7	23.4	11.4	35.8	29.4	14.9
Received inheritance	20.2	12.7	15.6	30.0	41.8	17.8	17.6	18.9	11.0	35.3	34.7	13.6

Table 4a. (Continued)

Determinants	Men						Women					
	Category Percentage	Still on a FTC Job	Moved to Self Employment	Moved to Wage & Salary	Out	SE (SE+WS+Out)	Category Percentage	Still on a FTC Job	Moved to Self Employment	Moved to Wage & Salary	Out	SE (SE+WS+Out)
Never received inheritance	79.8	13.4	10.2	33.3	43.1	11.8	82.4	21.8	7.6	34.8	35.8	9.7
Not married	10.5	13.3	8.3	31.1	47.2	9.6	25.3	13.9	8.1	37.5	40.5	9.4
Married	89.6	13.4	11.7	32.8	42.2	13.5	74.7	23.6	8.4	34.1	34.0	10.9
No dependent children	79.4	11.6	11.5	32.6	44.3	13.0	82.4	17.5	8.3	34.9	39.4	10.1
Dependent children	20.6	20.0	10.7	32.7	36.6	13.4	17.6	38.6	8.2	35.1	18.2	13.3
No employed spouse	39.5	13.1	10.4	30.6	45.9	12.0	41.6	17.0	8.3	35.4	39.3	10.0
Spouse employed	60.5	13.5	11.9	33.9	40.7	13.7	58.4	24.2	8.2	34.6	33.0	10.8
Spouse's health status												
excellent/ very good	58.1	12.4	13.9	32.4	41.3	15.9	53.0	24.2	8.4	35.3	32.1	11.1
good	27.5	14.5	9.9	32.7	42.9	11.6	29.4	21.7	8.0	35.8	34.5	10.2
fair/poor	14.4	15.7	5.6	34.3	44.4	6.6	17.5	25.1	7.8	27.7	39.4	10.4

Source: Authors' calculations based on data from the Health and Retirement Study.

To explore outcomes in more detail, we make use of the longitudinal nature of the HRS and categorize respondents according to their transitions from FTC jobs. Four general outcomes are possible by 2004: (1) remain on a FTC job, (2) move into self employment, (3) move into wage-and-salary employment, and (4) exit the labor force directly. Each of these outcomes is examined separately for those who were wage and salary on their FTC job and for those who were self employed (Table 3). The four-way outcome analysis results are consistent with the previous findings.[7] Those who were wage and salary on their FTC jobs were less likely to remain on their FTC jobs as of 2004 and more likely to exit directly from the labor force. Further, of those who were on a wage-and-salary FTC job in 1992 and who made a transition by 2004, about 12 percent of the men and 10 percent of the women had transitioned into a self- employment position. Among their counterparts who were self employed on their 1992 FTC job, about 42 percent of men and 39 percent of women transitioned to a wage-and-salary position.

Descriptive Statistics: Determinants

A key element of this research is to understand who transitions into self employment and why. To do so, we stratify the four-way outcome variable by various demographic and economic characteristics for the wage-and-salary and self-employed individuals separately. Among those who were wage and salary on the FTC job, we focus on the percentage who switched to self employment among those who made a transition (Tables 4a (demographic characteristics) and 5a (economic characteristics)). Among those who were self employed on the FTC job, we examine the percentage who switched to wage-and-salary jobs among those who made a transition (Tables 4b and 5b).

The major differences in who became self employed during a transition appear to be related to health status although, to a lesser extent, differences exist for other factors such as age, education, marital status, and spouse's employment status (Table 4a). Men who were wage and salary on their FTC job and who made a transition were much less likely to have become self employed if they were in fair or poor health. Approximately 4 percent of those in fair or poor health switched into self employment compared to 15 percent among those in excellent or very good health. Similar percentages were also associated with a spouse's health status. Another large discrepancy among men existed by educational status. Self-employment transitions were much more common among college-educated men than those who did not complete college (22 percent versus 10 percent). Further, self-employment transitions were somewhat more likely among men who were married and who had an employed spouse.

Women's transitions appeared similar to men's with respect to the impact of the set of demographic variables included in Table 4a. Two differences are of note. First, wage and salary women with dependent children were more likely to transition into self employment than those without dependent children. Second, rates of self employment were not impacted by a husband's health status.

Several findings regarding switches into wage-and-salary employment are worth mentioning. First, younger men were much more likely than older men to switch into wage-andsalary employment (Table 4b). Health status also positively impacted a switch into wage-andsalary employment, although differences were not as large as those found for switchers into self employment. Further, transitions from self employment to wage and salary employment were much more likely among men without a college degree, who were married, and who had a spouse in fair or poor health.

As with the findings regarding transitions into self employment, women with dependent children were more likely to switch employment status when making a transition. In contrast with the transition into self employment, however, women with a spouse in fair or poor health were more likely to switch into wage-and-salary employment.

The largest influence among the economic characteristics examined in this study pertained to wage rates and occupational status of the FTC job. Men who were wage-and-salary on their FTC jobs were much more likely to transition into self employment if they were high- wage earners (Table 5a). Fewer than ten percent of those who earned less than $10 per hour transitioned to a self-employed job, compared to about 18 percent of those who earned $20 to $50 per hour. About one half of those who earned $50 per hour or more on their wage-andsalary FTC job transitioned to a self-employed job. Occupational status was also a strong indicator of a transition into self employment. Approximately 20 percent of men with a white- collar, highly-skilled wage-and-salary FTC job transitioned to self employment, compared to about 5 percent of men with blue-collar, non-highly-skilled FTC jobs. Differences by health insurance status and pension status were not notable.

The impact of wage and occupational status was somewhat different for women on wage-and-salary jobs in 1992 than their male counterparts.

Table 4b. Transitions Out Of Self Employment as of 2004, by Demographic Characteristics Sample HRS Core Respondents on Self Employment FTC Jobs in Wave One.

Determinants	Men						Women					
	Category Percentage	Still on a FTC Job	Moved to Wage and Salary	Moved to Self Employed	Out	WS (SE+WS+Out)	Category Percentage	Still on a FTC Job	Moved to Wage and Salary	Moved to Self Employed	Out	WS (SE+WS+Out)
Age in 2004												
61 and younger	4.2%	27.8%	38.9%	22.2%	11.1%	53.8%	29.3%	29.5%	24.6%	32.8%	13.1%	34.9%
62 - 64	25.4	45.9	15.6	25.7	12.8	28.8	28.4	22.0	30.5	17.0	30.5	39.1
65 - 69	41.2	29.4	25.4	29.4	15.8	36.0	28.9	16.7	26.7	40.0	16.7	32.0
70 and older	29.3	12.7	26.2	40.5	20.6	30.0	13.5	7.1	32.1	42.9	17.9	34.6
Subjective health status												
excellent / very good	63.0	34.3	22.5	30.3	12.9	34.3	68.3	23.9	23.2	33.8	19.0	30.6
good	27.4	15.3	27.1	36.4	21.2	32.0	25.0	13.5	42.3	25.0	19.2	48.9
fair / poor	9.5	29.3	22.0	24.4	24.4	31.0	6.7	14.3	21.4	35.7	28.6	25.0
Less than college degree	70.5	29.4	24.8	29.4	16.5	35.0	84.6	18.2	28.4	32.4	21.0	34.7

Table 4b. (Continued)

Determinants	Men						Women					
	Category Percentage	Still on a FTC Job	Moved to Wage and Salary	Moved to Self Employed	Out	WS (SE+WS+Out)	Category Percentage	Still on a FTC Job	Moved to Wage and Salary	Moved to Self Employed	Out	WS (SE+WS+Out)
College degree	29.5	26.8	21.3	36.2	15.8	29.0	15.4	34.4	25.0	28.1	12.5	38.1
Received inheritance	27.3	18.0	29.1	39.3	13.7	35.4	24.0	20.0	24.0	40.0	16.0	30.0
Never received inheritance	72.7	32.7	21.8	28.2	17.3	32.4	76.0	20.9	29.1	29.1	20.9	36.8
Not married	9.3	22.5	22.5	35.0	20.0	29.0	17.8	18.9	29.7	32.4	18.9	36.7
Married	90.7	29.2	23.9	31.0	15.9	33.7	82.2	21.1	27.5	31.6	19.9	34.8
No dependent children	81.2	26.1	24.4	32.7	16.9	33.0	82.2	20.5	26.9	33.3	19.3	33.8
Dependent children	18.8	39.5	21.0	25.9	13.6	34.7	17.8	21.6	32.4	24.3	21.6	41.4
No employed spouse	37.0	24.5	24.5	35.2	15.7	32.5	33.7	21.4	27.1	25.7	25.7	34.5

Table 4b. (Continued)

Determinants	Men						Women					
	Category Percentage	Still on a FTC Job	Moved to Wage and Salary	Moved to Self Employed	Out	WS (SE+WS+Out)	Category Percentage	Still on a FTC Job	Moved to Wage and Salary	Moved to Self Employed	Out	WS (SE+WS+Out)
Spouse employed	63.0	31.0	23.3	29.2	16.6	33.7	66.4	20.3	28.3	34.8	16.7	35.5
Spouse's health status												
excellent / very good	68.5	31.6	21.7	31.2	15.6	31.7	57.4	20.4	29.0	35.5	15.1	36.4
good	21.1	28.4	24.7	30.9	16.1	34.4	21.0	20.6	17.7	35.3	26.5	22.3
fair / poor	10.4	12.5	37.5	32.5	17.5	42.9	21.6	22.9	31.4	22.9	22.9	40.7

Source: Authors' calculations based on data from the Health and Retirement Study.

Table 5a. Transitions Into Self Employment as of 2004, by Economic Characteristics Sample: HRS Core Respondents on Wage and Salary FTC Jobs in Wave One.

Determinants	Men						Women					
	Category Percentage	Still on a FTC Job	Moved to Self Employment	Moved to Wage & Salary	Out	SE (SE+WS+Out)	Category Percentage	Still on a FTC Job	Moved to Self Employment	Moved to Wage & Salary	Out	SE (SE+WS+Out)
Health insurance status												
Not covered on career job	5.0%	20.5%	10.3%	39.7%	29.5%	12.9%	7.4%	27.1%	17.0%	39.0%	17.0%	23.3%
"Covered, would maintain" coverage	81.2	11.2	11.7	32.0	45.1	13.2	80.2	19.0	6.9	36.1	38.0	8.5
"Covered, would lose" coverage	13.8	21.4	10.7	28.8	39.1	13.6	12.4	25.0	8.2	32.1	34.7	10.9
Pension status												
No pension	20.0	16.5	10.7	39.1	33.6	12.8	27.1	19.7	12.0	40.2	28.1	14.9
DC only	22.8	18.1	10.9	34.9	36.1	13.4	25.8	24.0	7.1	32.3	36.6	9.3
DB only	50.6	9.4	11.2	28.9	50.5	12.4	43.5	18.9	7.0	32.7	41.4	8.6
DC and DB	6.6	17.7	15.0	33.6	33.6	18.3	3.6	40.0	4.6	40.0	10.0	8.5

Table 5a. (Continued)

Determinants	Men						Women					
	Category Percentage	Still on a FTC Job	Moved to Self Employment	Moved to Wage & Salary	Out	SE (SE+WS+Out)	Category Percentage	Still on a FTC Job	Moved to Self Employment	Moved to Wage & Salary	Out	SE (SE+WS+Out)
Wage rate												
< $6/hour	5.4	15.1	7.0	46.5	31.4	8.2	12.3	28.0	8.1	39.8	24.2	11.2
$6 - $10/hour	17.5	16.4	7.5	36.4	39.6	9.0	35.2	21.4	8.5	34.6	35.6	10.8
$10 - $20/ hour	52.1	12.4	9.5	30.7	47.4	10.8	43.5	18.4	7.4	36.3	37.9	9.1
$20 - $50/ hour	23.8	11.5	16.2	31.9	40.3	18.3	8.8	26.0	9.3	29.3	35.3	12.6
> $50/hour	1.3	33.3	33.3	9.5	23.8	50.0	0.3	0.0	20.0	40.0	40.0	20.0
Occupation status												
White collar, highly skilled	34.5	14.4	16.1	32.0	37.6	18.8	35.0	22.9	9.6	34.8	32.7	12.5
White collar, other	12.8	15.5	13.2	33.2	38.2	15.6	37.3	22.5	6.4	35.7	35.5	8.2
Blue collar, highly skilled	40.5	10.2	8.6	32.2	48.9	9.6	12.3	13.0	5.8	35.0	46.2	6.7
Blue collar, other	12.2	19.1	4.3	34.5	42.1	5.3	15.4	20.8	11.8	33.7	33.7	14.9

Source: Authors' calculations based on data from the Health and Retirement Study.

Table 5b. Transitions Out of Self Employment as of 2004, by Economic Characteristics Sample: HRS Core Respondents on Self Employment FTC Jobs in Wave One.

Determinants	Men						Women					
	Category Percentage	Still on a FTC Job	Moved to Wage and Salary	Moved to Self Employed	Out	WS (SE+WS+Out)	Category Percentage	Still on a FTC Job	Moved to Wage and Salary	Moved to Self Employed	Out	WS (SE+WS+Out)
Health insurance status												
Not covered on career job	20.3%	25.0%	25.0%	37.5%	12.5%	33.3%	21.7%	12.5%	32.5%	32.5%	22.5%	37.1%
"Covered, would maintain" coverage	71.2	28.1	25.6	29.2	17.2	35.5	76.1	22.1	25.0	33.6	19.3	32.1
"Covered, would lose" coverage	8.1	35.5	16.1	25.8	22.6	25.0	2.2	25.0	50.0	0.0	25.0	66.7
Pension status												
No pension	58.4	28.9	20.1	32.3	18.7	28.2	85.6	21.4	25.3	31.5	21.9	32.1
DC only	12.6	31.5	35.2	24.1	9.3	51.4	7.2	26.7	33.3	26.7	13.3	45.5
DB only	14.2	31.2	23.0	34.4	11.5	33.3	6.7	7.1	50.0	42.9	0.0	53.8
DC and DB	4.9	9.5	47.6	28.6	14.3	52.6	0.5	----	----	----	----	----

Table 5b. (Continued)

Determinants	Men						Women					
	Category Percentage	Still on a FTC Job	Moved to Wage and Salary	Moved to Self Employed	Out	WS (SE+WS+Out)	Category Percentage	Still on a FTC Job	Moved to Wage and Salary	Moved to Self Employed	Out	WS (SE+WS+Out)
Wage rate												
< $6/hour	17.2	29.6	31.5	31.5	7.4	44.7	46.6	15.9	20.3	34.8	29.0	24.1
$6 - $10/hour	17.8	25.0	23.2	35.7	16.1	31.0	18.2	22.2	37.0	25.9	14.8	47.6
$10 - $20/ hour	33.1	31.7	22.1	29.8	16.4	32.4	19.6	27.6	27.6	34.5	10.3	38.1
$20 - $50/ hour	22.3	28.6	24.3	30.0	17.1	34.0	13.5	15.0	30.0	25.0	30.0	35.3
> $50/hour	9.6	30.0	16.7	33.3	20.0	23.8	2.0	----	----	----	----	----
Occupation status												
White collar, highly skilled	38.4	30.3	26.1	29.7	13.9	37.4	30.3	25.4	23.8	33.3	17.5	31.9
White collar, other	19.5	23.8	20.2	32.1	23.8	26.6	30.3	23.8	31.8	34.9	9.5	41.7
Blue collar, highly skilled	24.4	30.5	24.8	31.4	13.3	35.6	3.9	37.5	0.0	37.5	25.0	0.0
Blue collar, other	17.7	27.6	21.1	34.2	17.1	29.1	35.6	12.2	31.1	27.0	29.7	35.4

Source: Authors' calculations based on data from the Health and Retirement Study.

Differences by wage were smaller in magnitude, although the general trend was the same – those with higher wages were more likely to switch into self employment. In terms of occupation, women in blue-collar, non-highlyskilled jobs were more likely than those in white-collar, highly-skilled jobs to switch into self employment. Also unlike the male sample, differences existed by health insurance and pension status. Women without health insurance on their FTC job were much more likely than others to switch into self employment, as were those without pensions. This result should be interpreted with caution, however, because sample sizes were small.

Economic characteristics also appeared to influence transitions into wage-and-salary employment from self employment (Table 5b). Among men who were self employed on their FTC job and who made a transition, those who would lose their health insurance were less likely than others to switch to a wage-and-salary job. Another factor that positively influenced a switch to wage-and-salary employment was having a defined-contribution pension plan. Those with DC plans were much more likely to switch to wage-and-salary employment compared to those with DB pensions (51 percent versus 33 percent). Wages were generally not a strong influence on switching into wage-and-salary employment, although low wage workers were more likely than others to switch. Differences by occupational status existed as well, with those in highly- skilled white-collar and blue-collar jobs more likely to make a switch.

The number of observations for the female sample in several of the economic categories was too small to draw inferences; however, where observations were sufficient to examine outcomes, there were some findings of note. Women without pension coverage had a similar rate of switching into wage-and-salary employment as men without pensions. Unlike the men, though, low-wage women had the lowest prevalence of switching from self employment to wage-and-salary employment. Differences by occupational status did not follow any particular pattern.

Multivariate Analysis

This section examines transitions into self employment in a multivariate context. We estimate two self-employment models based on HRS respondents who were on a FTC wage-andsalary job in 1992 and for whom later employment status could be identified. The first specification is one in which self employment is viewed as a dichotomous decision. The dependent variable is equal to one if a worker who was on a FTC wage-and-salary job in 1992 ever transitioned into self employment between 1992 and 2004, and equal to zero otherwise. The second specification examines transitions from wage-and-salary FTC jobs in more detail, using the four-way dependent variable presented earlier in Tables 4 and 5. The outcomes are defined as of 2004 and are as follows: (1) remained on a FTC job, (2) moved to a different wageand-salary job, (3) moved to a self-employed job, and (4) exited the labor force directly from a FTC job. The coefficients of each model are estimated for men and women separately using logistic regression for the first model and multinomial logistic regression for the second model.

The multivariate analysis generally confirms the descriptive findings. Among men, the logistic regression results show that respondents in fair or poor health or respondents with spouses in fair or poor health were about five percentage point less likely than otherwise similar respondents to switch from wage-and-salary FTC jobs to self employment (Table 6a). Occupational status was also a strong predictor of self-employment transitions, with white-collar, highly-skilled workers the most likely to switch into self employment. Pension status was also marginally significant, as those without a pension on the FTC job were more likely to switch into self employment.

The logistic regression for the female sample revealed fewer statistically-significant coefficients, but those that were significant appeared consistent with the findings for the male sample (Table 6b). Two coefficients were significant among women that were not significant for men. The lack of health insurance appeared to be positively associated with switching into self employment, all else equal, and home ownership was negatively associated with switching into self employment (after controlling for wealth). One observation of note is that, like the descriptive statistics, occupational status was not a significant predictor of switching into self employment among women.

The multinomial logistic regressions reinforced many of the descriptive findings and the logistic regression results. Again, the main drivers of post-FTC transitions were age, health status, occupational status, and pension status. Among men, younger respondents were more likely to switch to a different wage-and-salary job and older men were more likely to exit the labor force directly (Table 7a). Those in fair or poor health were less likely to take a self- employed job after FTC wage-and-salary employment and were more likely to exit the labor force directly. Blue-collar workers were less likely than white-collar workers to take either a different wage-and-salary or a self-employed job after FTC wage-and-salary employment and were more likely to exit directly. Sample sizes for women appear to have limited the extent to which statistical significance could be found. Two findings from the logistic regression remain, however; women without health insurance and without pensions were less likely to exit the labor force directly than otherwise similar women (Table 7b).

Table 6a. Marginal Effects from Logistic Regression Dependent Variable: Switch to Self Employment by 2004 Sample: Men on Wage & Salary FTC Jobs in 1992.

	coef	p-value
Age in 1992		
54 or younger	—	—
55 - 59	-0.009	0.499
60 or older	0.002	0.900
Respondent health		
Excellent/very good	0.005	0.740
Good	—	—
Fair/poor	-0.048	0.067
Spouse health		
Excellent/very good	0.0 17	0.257
Good	—	—
Fair/poor	-0.048	0.067
College graduate	0.023	0.162
Married	0.006	0.805
Dependent child	-0.00 1	0.972
Spouse employed	-0.002	0.875
Occupational status		
Blue collar - high skilled	-0.040	0.022
Blue collar - other	-0.05 8	0.03 8
White collar - high skilled	—	—
White collar - other	-0.0 13	0.500
Health insurance status		
Portable	-0.012	0.406
Non-portable	—	—
None	0.017	0.577
Pension status		
Defined-benefit	-0.030	0.071
Defined-contribution	-0.03 8	0.048
Both	-0.030	0.283
None	—	—
Own home	-0.005	0.80 1
Constant	-0.164	0.000

Source: Authors' calculations based on data from the Health and Retirement Study.

Note: Logistic regression also controls for race, wage, wage squared, wealth, wealth squared, receipt of an inheritance, and region.

Table 6b. Marginal Effects from Logistic Regression Dependent Variable: Switch to Self Employment by 2004 Sample: Women on Wage & Salary FTC Jobs in 1992.

	coef	p-value
Age in 1992		
54 or younger	—	—
55 - 59	-0.005	0.675
60 or older	0.002	0.918
Respondent health		
Excellent/very good	0.020	0.09 1
Good	—	—
Fair/poor	-0.030	0.149
Spouse health		
Excellent/very good	-0.003	0.802
Good	—	—
Fair/poor	-0.005	0.786
College graduate	0.0 13	0.4 15
Married	0.002	0.903
Dependent child	-0.004	0.775
Spouse employed	0.002	0.85 1
Occupational status		
Blue collar - high skilled	-0.0 13	0.50 1
Blue collar - other	0.0 12	0.489
White collar - high skilled	—	—
White collar - other	-0.011	0.432
Health insurance status		
Portable	0.011	0.3 50
Non-portable	—	—
None	0.03 6	0.031
Pension status		
Defined-benefit	-0.035	0.002
Defined-contribution	-0.03 8	0.004
Both	-0.066	0.061
None	—	—
Own home	-0.024	0.059
Constant	-0.169	0.000

Source: Authors' calculations based on data from the Health and Retirement Study.

Note: Logistic regression also controls for race, wage, wage squared, wealth, wealth squared, receipt of an inheritance, and region.

Table 7a. Marginal Effects from Multinomial Logistic Regression Dependent Variable: First Transition from Full-Time Career Job Men on a Full-Time Career Job in 1992.

	Wage & Salary Bridge Job		Self Employed Bridge Job		Exit the Labor Force	
	coef	p-value	coef	p-value	coef	p-value
Age in 1992						
54 or younger	—	—	—	—	—	—
55 - 59	-0.109	0.000	0.001	0.933	0.178	0.000
60 or older	-0.124	0.000	0.003	0.866	0.263	0.000
Respondent health						
Excellent/very good	0.029	0.257	-0.006	0.694	-0.039	0.155
Good	—	—	—	—	—	—
Fair/poor	-0.034	0.388	-0.071	0.017	0.159	0.000
Spouse health						
Excellent/very good	0.000	0.990	0.018	0.257	0.001	0.977
Good	—	—	—	—	—	—
Fair/poor	0.025	0.507	-0.018	0.513	-0.020	0.635
College	-0.022	0.535	0.017	0.332	-0.044	0.240
Married	0.026	0.539	-0.006	0.817	-0.051	0.267
Dependent child	-0.020	0.475	-0.007	0.703	0.005	0.880
Spouse employed	0.017	0.503	0.010	0.524	-0.029	0.302
Occupational status						
Blue collar-high skilled	-0.082	0.010	-0.044	0.016	0.155	0.000
Blue collar-other	-0.074	0.098	-0.079	0.012	0.131	0.008
White collar-high skilled	—	—	—	—	—	—
White collar- other	-0.026	0.505	-0.019	0.354	0.042	0.320
Health insurance status						
Portable	0.040	0.102	-0.03 1	0.038	-0.006	0.83 1
Non-portable	—	—	—	—	—	—
None	0.051	0.348	0.023	0.489	-0.075	0.213
Pension status						
Defined-benefit	-0.083	0.007	-0.017	0.341	0.125	0.000
Defined-contribution	-0.014	0.683	-0.026	0.212	0.001	0.970
Both	-0.017	0.738	-0.003	0.927	-0.003	0.963
None	—	—	—	—	—	—
Own home	-0.054	0.105	0.002	0.925	0.063	0.090
Constant	0.196	0.005	-0.066	0.092	-0.069	0.363

Source: Authors' calculations based on data from the Health and Retirement Study.

Note: Multinomial logistic regression also controls for race, wage, wage squared, wealth, wealth squared, receipt of an inheritance, and region.

V. CONCLUSION

Self employment among the working population increases substantially as workers approach retirement age. According to data from the Health and Retirement Study, about 20 percent of men aged 51 to 61 in 1992 were self employed, already a sizable proportion. Twelve years later, more than one third of those working were self employed – an increase of more than 50 percent. Among older women, the increase in self employment was from about 10 percent to more than 15 percent. The rise in self employment later in life is a result of a combination of factors, including the fact that self-employed workers tend to stay in the labor force longer than wage-and-salary workers and that more wage-and-salary workers switch into self employment later in life than vice versa. Some of the key determinants of these transitions included health status, spouse's health status, educational attainment, and occupational status.

The degree to which older Americans switch from wage-and-salary employment to self employment is an interesting outcome. The implication is that self-employment decisions are not predetermined during middle age; in fact, it is just the opposite. Older workers exhibit a great deal of flexibility in their work decisions and appear willing to take on substantial risks later in life. In a sense, the outcome is intuitive, as older workers are more likely than younger workers to have access to investment capital. Their lifetime of experience may also help them avoid many of the pitfalls associated with running a business that may ensnare younger, less experienced workers.

Policymakers and employers may have a lot to gain by understanding the self- employment transitions of older Americans, because the decision to remain working later in life is likely linked to the type of work people will be doing. Self employment, for example, provides many older workers with the flexibility that they desire in a work schedule. If needs such as these are met, many older workers may continue to work later in life and be a valuable resource as the population ages.

Table 7b. Marginal Effects from Multinomial Logistic Regression Dependent Variable: First Transition from Full-Time Career Job Women on a Full-Time Career Job in 1992.

	Wage & Salary Bridge Job		Self Employed Bridge Job		Exit the Labor Force	
	coef	p-value	coef	p-value	coef	p-value
Age in 1992						
54 or younger	—	—	—	—	—	—
55 - 59	-0.018	0.507	-0.002	0.899	0.180	0.000
60 or older	-0.05 1	0.356	0.009	0.705	0.345	0.000
Respondent health						
Excellent/very good	0.03 1	0.266	0.027	0.053	-0.113	0.000
Good	—	—	—	—	—	—
Fair/poor	-0.059	0.196	-0.021	0.388	0.144	0.001
Spouse health						
Excellent/very good	-0.014	0.652	0.004	0.788	0.005	0.885
Good	—	—	—	—	—	—
Fair/poor	-0.097	0.025	0.009	0.649	0.074	0.079
College	0.029	0.430	0.011	0.545	-0.057	0.120
Married	-0.017	0.679	-0.003	0.876	-0.032	0.463
Dependent child	0.085	0.013	0.005	0.766	-0.192	0.000
Spouse employed	-0.022	0.509	0.000	0.983	0.032	0.348
Occupational status						
Blue collar-high skilled	-0.002	0.96 1	-0.006	0.769	0.084	0.064
Blue collar-other	-0.024	0.596	0.027	0.177	0.006	0.891
White collar-high skilled	—	—	—	—	—	—
White collar-other	0.007	0.825	-0.021	0.234	0.025	0.449
Health insurance status						
Portable	0.042	0.103	0.008	0.542	-0.017	0.512
Non-portable	—	—	—	—	—	—
None	0.080	0.124	0.049	0.012	-0.135	0.022
Pension status						
Defined-benefit	-0.098	0.001	-0.020	0.133	0.106	0.001
Defined-contribution	-0.089	0.008	-0.023	0.137	0.056	0.104
Both	0.064	0.354	-0.060	0.179	-0.122	0.119
None	—	—	—	—	—	—
Own home	-0.007	0.831	-0.027	0.075	0.056	0.115
Constant	0.205	0.003	-0.118	0.000	-0.064	0.362

Source: Authors' calculations based on data from the Health and Retirement Study.

Note: Multinomial logistic regression also controls for race, wage, wage squared, wealth, wealth squared, receipt of an inheritance, and region.

References

[1] Bruce, D., Holtz-Eakin, D. & Quinn, J. (2000). Self-Employment and Labor Market Transitions at Older Ages. Center for Retirement Research at Boston College Working Paper 2000-13. Retrieved February 15, 2007 from_http://www.bc.edu/centers/crr/papers/wp_2000-13.pdf

[2] Burkhauser, R. & Quinn, J. F. (1997). Implementing Pro-Work Policies for Older Americans in the Twenty-First Century. *Preparing for the Baby-Boomers: The Role of Employment. U.S. Special Committee on Aging,* Serial Number 105-7, 60-83.

[3] Cahill, K. E., Giandrea, M. D. & Quinn, J. F. (2006). Retirement Patterns from Career Employment. *The Gerontologist, 46(4),* 514-523.

[4] Dunn, T. & Holtz-Eakin, D. (2000). Financial Capital, Human Capital, and the Transition to Self-Employment: Evidence from Intergenerational Links. *Journal of Labor Economics, 18(2),* 282-305.

[5] Evans, D. S. & Jovanovic, B. (1989). An estimated model of entrepreneurial choice under liquidity constraints. *The Journal of Political Economy*, *97(4),* 808-827.

[6] Fuchs, V. R. (1982). Self-Employment and Labor Force Participation of Older Males. *The Journal of Human Resources, 17(3),* 339-357.

[7] Hamilton, B. H. (2000). Does Entrepreneurship Pay? An Empirical Analysis of the Returns of Self-Employment. *The Journal of Political Economy, 108(3),* 604-631.

[8] Hipple, S. (2004). Self-employment in the United States: an update. *Monthly Labor Review, 127(7),* 13-23.

[9] Holtz-Eakin, D., Joulfaian, D. & Rosen, H. S. (1994a). Sticking it Out: Entrepreneurial Survival and Liquidity Constraints. *The Journal of Political Economy, 102(1),* 53-75.

[10] Holtz-Eakin, D., Joulfaian, D. & Rosen, H. S. (1994b). Entrepreneurial Decisions and Liquidity Constraints. *The RAND Journal of Economics, 25(2),* 334-347.

[11] Juster, F. T. & Suzman, R. (1995). An Overview of the Health and Retirement Study. *Journal of Human Resources*, *30*(Supplement), S7-S56.

[12] Lettau, M. K. (1997). Compensation in Part-Time versus Full-Time Jobs: What if the Job is the Same? *Economics Letters, Vol.* 56, *101-106.*

[13] Penner, R. G., Perun, P. & Steuerle, E. (2002). Legal and Institutional Impediments to Partial Retirement and Part-Time Work by Older Workers. Urban Institute. Retrieved from http://www.urban

[14] Social Security Administration Fact Sheet downloaded April 11, 2007 from http://www.ssa.gov/pressoffice/factsheets/basicfact-alt.pdf

[15] Zissimopoulos, J., Maestas, N. & Karoly, L. (2007). The Effect of Retirement Incentives on Retirement Behavior: Evidence from the Self-Employed in the United States and England. University of Michigan Retirement Research Center, WP 2007-155.

End Notes

[1] See Burkhauser and Quinn (1997).
[2] See Cahill, Giandrea, and Quinn (2006).
[3] See Hipple (2004).
[4] See Social Security Administration Fact Sheet (2007).
[5] Branchflower and Oswald (1998) found that self-employed workers exhibited higher levels of both job and life satisfaction than wage-and-salary employees.
[6] See Juster and Suzman (1995) for a detailed description of the HRS.
[7] See Cahill et al. (2006)

In: Older Workers Navigating Employment and... ISBN: 978-1-61470-253-5
Editors: Benjamin V. Chase

Chapter 5

THE AGE DISCRIMINATION IN EMPLOYMENT ACT (ADEA): A LEGAL OVERVIEW

Jody Feder

SUMMARY

This report provides an overview of the Age Discrimination in Employment Act (ADEA) and discusses current legal and legislative developments. The ADEA, which prohibits employment discrimination against persons over the age of 40, was enacted "to promote employment of older persons based on their ability rather than age; to prohibit arbitrary age discrimination in employment; [and] to help employers and workers find ways of meeting problems arising from the impact of age on employment."

The ADEA, which applies to employers, labor organizations, and employment agencies, makes it unlawful for an employer "to fail or refuse to hire or to discharge any individual or otherwise discriminate against any individual with respect to his compensation, terms, conditions, or privileges of employment, because of such individual's age." The statute not only applies to hiring, discharge, and promotion, but also prohibits discrimination in employee benefit plans such as health coverage and pensions. The Equal Employment Opportunity Commission (EEOC) is responsible for enforcing the provisions of the ADEA.

The ADEA applies to employers who have "twenty or more employees for each working day in each of twenty or more calendar weeks in the current or preceding calendar year." A labor organization is covered by the ADEA if it "exists for the purpose ... of dealing with employers concerning grievances, labor disputes, wages, rates of pay, hours, or other terms or conditions of employment." An employment agency and its agents are subject to the ADEA if the agency "regularly undertakes with or without compensation" the procurement of employees for an employer, other than an agency of the United States. The ADEA also covers congressional and most federal employees.

I. INTRODUCTION

The Age Discrimination in Employment Act (ADEA) of 1967,[1] as amended, seeks to address the longstanding problem of age discrimination in the workplace. The ADEA, which prohibits employment discrimination against persons over the age of 40, was enacted "to promote employment of older persons based on their ability rather than age; to prohibit arbitrary age discrimination in employment; [and] to help employers and workers find ways of meeting problems arising from the impact of age on employment."[2] The ADEA makes it unlawful for an employer "to fail or refuse to hire or to discharge any individual or otherwise discriminate against any individual with respect to his compensation, terms, conditions, or privileges of employment, because of such individual's age."[3] The statute not only applies to hiring, discharge, and promotion, but also prohibits discrimination in employee benefit plans such as health coverage and pensions. In addition to employers, the ADEA also applies to labor organizations and employment agencies.

After it was enacted, the ADEA went through a series of amendments to strengthen and expand its coverage of older employees. Originally, the ADEA only covered employees between the ages of 40 and 65. Eventually the upper age limit was extended to age 70, and then eliminated altogether. In 1978, enforcement authority of the ADEA was transferred from the Department of Labor to the Equal Employment Opportunity Commission (EEOC).[4]

II. Requirements Under the ADEA

Coverage

Employers

The ADEA applies to employers who have "twenty or more employees for each working day in each of twenty or more calendar weeks in the current or preceding calendar year."[5] Companies that are incorporated in a foreign country but that are controlled by a U.S. employer are subject to the ADEA, and U.S. citizens employed by a U.S. employer to work in a foreign country are also covered, unless compliance with the ADEA would violate the laws of that country.[6] The determination regarding whether a company is under an American employer's control is based on the interrelation of operations, common management, centralized control of labor relations, and common ownership or financial control between the employer and the corporation.[7]

Although the statutory definition of "employer" technically excludes the United States, a separate ADEA provision extends coverage to federal employees in certain military departments, executive agencies, the United States Postal Service, the Postal Rate Commission, certain District of Columbia agencies, federal legislative and judicial branch units with positions in the competitive service, the Smithsonian Institution, the Government Printing Office, the General Accounting Office, and the Library of Congress.[8] Congressional employees of the House and Senate are also covered by the ADEA pursuant to the Congressional Accountability Act of 1995.[9] In addition, the term "employer" includes state and local governments.[10]

Despite the fact that the ADEA applies to state governments, the United States Supreme Court in *Kimel v. Florida Board of Regents* held that state employees could not sue states for monetary damages under the ADEA.[11] The Court reasoned that states have sovereign immunity and are immune from suit unless the state consents or an exception applies. While, the *Kimel* decision effectively eliminated the ability of state employees to bring suit for monetary damages against states under the ADEA, the act may still be enforced against states by the EEOC, and state employees may still sue state officials for declaratory and injunctive relief.

In addition to employers, labor organizations and employment agencies are also subject to the ADEA. A labor organization is covered by the ADEA if it "exists for the purpose ... of dealing with employers concerning grievances, labor disputes, wages, rates of pay, hours, or other terms or conditions of employment."[12] The ADEA defines a labor organization as an entity that has a hiring hall or is a certified employee representative, or if not certified, holds itself out as the employee's bargaining representative.[13] Meanwhile, an employment agency and its agents are subject to the ADEA if the agency "regularly undertakes with or without compensation" to provide employees for an employer.[14]

Employees

In general, the ADEA covers employees who are forty years of age and older.[15] Because the statute prohibits discrimination against individuals regarding any terms or conditions of employment, the act's protections not only cover employees but also extend to both applicants for employment and discharged ex-employees. Both private and public employees are generally covered by the ADEA. For example, the ADEA applies to most federal employees, and the Congressional Accountability Act of 1995 extended the rights and protections of the ADEA to congressional employees.[16] State elected officials and their personal staff, appointees, and legal advisers are excluded from the definition of employee, although state employees covered by civil service laws are considered employees.

Despite the ADEA's exemption for the personal staff, appointees, and legal advisers of state officials, such individuals may nevertheless be able to file age discrimination claims under a separate law, the Government Employee Rights Act.[17] State officials remain exempt and therefore are not protected from age discrimination by either law.[18]

The ADEA contains several notable exceptions to the prohibition against age discrimination. For example, although mandatory retirement policies generally constitute a violation of the ADEA, the statute permits employers to establish compulsory retirement for a bona fide executive or high policymaker who has reached age 65 and is entitled to a pension benefit of at least $44,000.[19] Under certain circumstances, state and local governments may establish mandatory retirement requirements for their firefighters or law enforcement officers.[20] Also exempt are federal civil service employees who are air traffic controllers, firefighters, law enforcement officers, nuclear materials couriers, and customs and border protection officers.[21]

Although the ADEA did at one point contain an exception for tenured faculty at institutions of higher education, that exception has expired. Currently, however, the ADEA does allow institutions of higher education to offer tenured employees who become eligible to retire "supplemental benefits" to encourage them to voluntarily retire. Supplemental benefits are those benefits above and beyond retirement or severance benefits generally offered to employees of the institution. If certain requirements are met, supplemental benefits may be reduced or eliminated on the basis of age without violating the ADEA. However, the ADEA continues to prohibit an institution from reducing or ceasing non-supplemental benefits on the basis of age.[22]

Prohibited Acts

As noted above, the ADEA applies to a broad range of employment practices, including discrimination because of age in hiring, placement, promotion, demotion, transfer, termination, and discipline. Because the statute prohibits age discrimination with respect to all terms and conditions of employment, discrimination regarding salary, leave, and other benefits may also violate the act. In addition, the statute prohibits discrimination in referrals by employment agencies, actions by unions, and retaliation against employees for filing or participating in an ADEA claim or for opposing an employer's discriminatory practices.[23]

Although the ADEA expressly prohibits retaliation in the private sector, the statute is less clear with regard to retaliation involving age discrimination in the federal sector. In 2008, the Supreme Court addressed this issue in *Gomez-Perez v. Potter*, holding that the ADEA does indeed prohibit retaliation in federal employment.[24] Relying on precedents established in cases involving other anti-discrimination statutes, the Court ruled that a prohibition against retaliation is encompassed within the general prohibition against age discrimination in the federal sector.

Because the statute covers individuals who are age forty or older, younger employees are not protected from age discrimination. Indeed, employers may engage in so-called reverse discrimination—favoring employees over the age of forty—without violating the statute. Furthermore, the Supreme Court has held that the ADEA does not prohibit employers from discriminating against employees who are protected under the statute in favor of older members of the protected class.[25] According to the Court, although the ADEA "forbids discriminatory preference for the young over the old," it does not prohibit favoring the old over the young, even when the younger and older employees are within the protected class, i.e., age forty or older.[26] In contrast, the Court has separately held that the ADEA does prohibit discrimination against older employees in favor of younger employees who are older than forty years old.[27]

Before entering an employment relationship with their workers, most employers advertise the job opening. As a result, such advertisements are subject to the ADEA, which prohibits advertisements that contain age preferences unless age is a bona fide occupational qualification for the position advertised.[28] According to the EEOC's regulations, advertisements that contain phrases such as, "age 25 to 35," "young," "college student," "recent college graduate," "boy," "girl," or similar terms are prohibited under the act, unless an exception applies. Even phrases that favor some members of the class, but discriminate against others is prohibited, such as "age 40 to 50," "age over 65," "retired person," or "supplement your pension."[29] On the other hand, the request for the age or date of birth of an applicant on an employment application or use of the phrase "state age" on a want ad is not automatically a violation because there may be legitimate reasons for requesting the age or date of birth of an applicant.[30] However, the EEOC will "closely [scrutinize the application] to assure that the request is for a permissible purpose and not for purposes proscribed by the Act."[31]

Defenses and Exceptions

The ADEA provides several defenses for employers. These available defenses attempt to strike a balance between the ability of employers to conduct their business and the interest of the government in eliminating age discrimination in employment.

Under one prominent exception, an employer will not be deemed to have violated the act when the action taken against an employee is due to a "bona fide occupational qualification [BFOQ] reasonably necessary to the normal operation of the particular business."[32] According to the Supreme Court, the BFOQ must be more than "convenient" or "reasonable," but must be "'reasonably necessary ... to the particular business.'"[33] Under this narrow interpretation, an employer must justify an age-based employment requirement by demonstrating (1) that the requirement is reasonably necessary to the essence of its business, and (2) that an individualized approach would be pointless or impractical. The second prong of this test can be established in one of two ways. First the employer may show that it had a factual basis for believing that persons over a certain age would be unable to perform the job safely. In the alternative, the employer may show that "age was a legitimate proxy for the safety-related job qualifications by proving that it is 'impossible or highly impractical' to deal with the older employees on an individualized basis."[34] Although employers have attempted to use the BFOQ defense in a wide variety of occupations, job-related age requirements have tended to be more successful when the position in question, such as airline pilot or law enforcement officer, may affect public safety.

Another defense to a charge of age discrimination may apply if "the differentiation is based on reasonable factors other than age [RFOTA]."[35] Similarly, disciplining or discharging an employee for good cause also constitutes a defense to the act.[36] In both of these defenses, an employer asserts that its adverse action did not involve age discrimination but rather was based on some other factor. Such factors may include job performance, business cutbacks, or lack of qualifications, among others. In addition, the Court has held that employers may, without violating the ADEA, make employment decisions based on cost factors that are highly correlated with age, such as pensions or high salaries, as long as their actions are not actually based on age.[37] Indeed, in *Kentucky Retirement Systems v. Equal Employment Opportunity Commission*,[38] the Supreme Court upheld a state retirement plan that imputed additional years of service to employees who became disabled before becoming eligible for retirement at age 55, but did not, for purposes of calculating pensions, impute additional years of service to employees who became disabled after they became eligible for retirement. The Court ultimately held that the retirement plan, which treated employees differently based on their pension status, was designed to provide pension benefits to disabled employees and was not "actually motivated" by age. Thus, the Court ruled that the retirement plan did not violate the ADEA.

Under the ADEA, it is also permissible for an employer to take action pursuant to a bona fide seniority system or employee benefit plan, although neither the seniority system nor the benefit plan may require mandatory retirement of employees because of age.[39] However, the ADEA explicitly allows voluntary early retirement as an incentive of employee benefit plans. In addition, a bona fide employee benefit plan must satisfy the "equal cost equal benefit" principle that provides parity between the amount employers spend on benefits for older and younger workers.[40] If it costs more to provide the same benefit to the protected class, the employer has the option of paying the same amount for benefits of the protected class as it does for employees outside of the protected class. This is so, even if it results in workers in the protected class receiving fewer benefits. However, employers may not pay less for benefits of members of the protected class than they pay for younger employees.

In recent years, there has been a debate over the extent to which the "equal benefits or equal costs" principle should be applied to retired employees. In order to cut costs, some employers have sought to provide one level of health benefits to retirees under age 65 to cover them until they are eligible for Medicare and then reduce or eliminate the benefit when the retiree becomes Medicare eligible. In *Erie County Retirees Ass'n v. County of Erie*,[41] the Court of Appeals for the Third Circuit ruled that the ADEA applies to retirees and held that the practice of providing different benefits to older and younger retirees based on their eligibility for Medicare constitutes age discrimination in violation of the act because Medicare eligibility is an "explicitly" age-related factor. Fearing that employers might reduce or eliminate benefits for all retirees rather than increase benefits for older, Medicare-eligible retirees, the EEOC, which exercised its statutory authority to approve reasonable exceptions to the ADEA,[42] promulgated a rule stating that it is not a violation of the act to alter, reduce, or eliminate health benefits for retirees when the participant becomes eligible for Medicare or comparable state health benefits.[43]

Finally, as noted above, the ADEA permits employers to impose mandatory retirement with respect to certain categories of employees, such as executives and high policymakers, as well as firefighters and law enforcement officers.

Disparate Treatment vs. Disparate Impact

When bringing a civil case alleging employment discrimination, there are two types of claims that a plaintiff can make: disparate treatment and disparate impact. Disparate treatment occurs when an employer intentionally discriminates against an employee or enacts a policy with the intent to treat or affect the employee differently from others because of the employee's age. Such disparate treatment claims require proof that the employer intended to discriminate against the complaining party when it took the challenged employment action. Intent, the critical element of a disparate treatment claim, may be shown directly (e.g., by discriminatory statements or behavior of a supervisor towards a subordinate) or, perhaps more likely, by circumstantial evidence.

Meanwhile, disparate impact occurs when the employer's acts or policies are facially neutral, but have an adverse impact on a class of employees and are not otherwise reasonable. Unlike disparate treatment claims, disparate impact claims may be established without proof of discriminatory intent, relieving the victim of an often insurmountable burden. Although the ADEA clearly allows disparate treatment claims, it was, for many years, unclear whether an employee may recover under a disparate impact theory, which led to confusion for litigants and lower courts alike.[44] In 2005, however, the Supreme Court held in *Smith v. City of Jackson* that the ADEA does indeed authorize disparate impact claims.[45]

Over the years, the courts have developed a complicated set of rules and procedures that govern how disparate treatment and disparate impact claims are adjudicated. Many of the cases in which these rules have evolved are Title VII cases, but their reasoning typically applies in the ADEA context as well. These rules, which differ depending on the type of claim involved, are discussed below.

Proving a Disparate Treatment Claim

In general, the courts evaluate individual disparate treatment claims under the ADEA in one of two ways.[46] When direct evidence of discrimination is lacking, plaintiffs are generally subject to the burden-shifting framework established by the Supreme Court in *McDonnell Douglas v. Green* and *Texas Dept. of Community Affairs v. Burdine*.[47] When the plaintiff has direct evidence of age discrimination, use of the *McDonnell Douglas* burden-shifting model may be unnecessary.[48]

Under the *McDonnell Douglas* burden-shifting framework, a plaintiff must first establish a prima facie case, meaning that a plaintiff must allege facts that are adequate to support a legal claim.

Once a plaintiff, by a preponderance of the evidence, establishes a prima facie case, then the burden of production shifts to the employer, "to articulate some legitimate, nondiscriminatory reason for the employee's rejection."[49] If the employer successfully rebuts the employee's prima facie case by articulating such a reason, then the employee may still prevail if he can show that the employer's defense is merely a pretext and that the employer's behavior was actually motivated by discrimination.[50] While the burden of production shifts to the employer to rebut the employee's prima facie case, the burden of persuasion remains on the plaintiff at all times.[51]

Because the *McDonnell Douglas* framework was originally established in a Title VII case involving failure to hire, there has been some confusion among the courts when applying this model to ADEA claims, particularly when it comes to defining what constitutes a prima facie case of age discrimination. Under the facts in the *McDonnell Douglas* case, a prima facie case would be established when the plaintiff showed: "(1) that he belongs to a racial minority; (2) that he applied and was qualified for a job for which the employer was seeking applicants; (3) that, despite his qualifications, he was rejected; and (4) that, after his rejection, the position remained open and the employer continued to seek applicants from persons of complainant's qualifications."[52] As adapted to the ADEA context, therefore, a plaintiff generally must show that he or she is a member of the protected age group, that he or she was adversely affected by an employment action, and that such action was taken because of the employee's age in order to establish a prima facie case of age discrimination.[53] However, because the elements of a prima facie case may vary somewhat depending on the type of employment action that was taken (e.g., failure to hire, discharge, demotion, compensation, etc.), a plaintiff may have to make additional—or more specific—showings in order to establish a prima facie case.[54]

As noted above, if an employer rebuts the plaintiff's prima facie case by offering a legitimate nondiscriminatory reason for its employment action, then the plaintiff must establish that the employer's reason is a pretext for discrimination. A plaintiff may show pretext in a variety of ways, such as offering statistical evidence, proof of discriminatory statements by an employer, or evidence of harassment, although presentation of such evidence does not guarantee that the plaintiff will be successful. In addition, a plaintiff may, in some cases, demonstrate pretext by offering evidence of discrimination against other employees. Indeed, in *Sprint/United Management Company v. Mendelsohn*,[55] the plaintiff attempted to introduce testimony by several former employees who claimed they had suffered age discrimination at the hands of their supervisors, even though those supervisors worked in another part of the company and were not involved in any discriminatory action taken against the plaintiff. Noting that "[t]he question whether evidence of discrimination by other supervisors is relevant in an individual ADEA case is fact based and depends on many factors," the Supreme Court held that such evidence is neither per se admissible nor per se inadmissible and therefore the district court should determine the admissibility of such evidence on a case by case basis.[56] Because many lower courts had been excluding such evidence, the Court's decision is expected to benefit employees who want to introduce co-worker evidence in future cases.

Until recently, another type of disparate treatment claim was available to plaintiffs under the ADEA. Originally recognized by the Court in the Title VII *Price Waterhouse v. Hopkins* case,[57] "mixed-motive" claims involve employment actions that are based on both discriminatory and nondiscriminatory reasons. Such claims generally follow a different method of proof.[58] In 2009, however, the Court decided *Gross v. FBL Financial Services, Inc.*,[59] a case in which the Court evaluated what types of evidence the parties must present and who bears the burden of proof in mixed-motive ADEA cases. Sidestepping the evidentiary question presented, the Court determined that an employer never bears the burden of persuasion because the traditional mixed-motive burden-shifting framework is not applicable to the ADEA. Finding instead that the ADEA does not authorize the type of mixed-motive claims that are available under Title VII, the Court held that an employee in a mixed-motive case bears the burden of establishing that "age was the 'but-for' cause of the challenged adverse employment action,"[60] meaning that the employee must show that age was the deciding factor, rather than just one of several motivating factors, behind the employer's action. This standard is likely to make it more difficult for plaintiffs to succeed in age discrimination cases in which age is only one of several factors behind the adverse employment decision.[61]

Proving a Disparate Impact Claim

As noted above, the Supreme Court has clarified that plaintiffs may bring disparate impact claims under the ADEA, reasoning that the ADEA is analogous to Title VII, under which disparate impact claims are authorized.[62] The process for bringing such claims, however, differs from the process for proving a disparate treatment claim. In addition, because of differences between the ADEA and Title VII, plaintiffs who decide to pursue disparate impact claims under the ADEA must comply with rules of proof that differ from the rules that govern disparate impact claims under Title VII.

In order to bring a disparate impact claim under the ADEA, a plaintiff must first establish a prima facie case of age discrimination by demonstrating that a given employment practice has a disparate impact on members of the protected class. At this stage, a plaintiff must identify the specific employment practice that is responsible for the disparate impact.[63] The employer may then rebut the prima facie case by showing that the adverse impact was attributable to a reasonable factor other than age, a requirement based on the statutory provision that exempts otherwise prohibited employment actions that are based on a reasonable factor other than age.

Until recently, there was confusion among the federal courts regarding the question of whether it is the employee or employer who bears the burden of demonstrating that the challenged employment practice is reasonable or unreasonable. In *Meacham v. Knolls Atomic Power Laboratory*, the Supreme Court ruled that the employer is responsible for proving that its action was in fact reasonable.[64] The Court's decision rested in part on its determination that the party who claims the benefits of a statutory exception must bear the burden of proving its actions were justified.[65] Ultimately, the result in the *Meacham* case appears to make it easier for plaintiffs to prevail in disparate impact cases.

Enforcement and Filing Procedures

The EEOC is responsible for enforcing the provisions of the ADEA.[66] In order to encourage informal resolution of age discrimination disputes, the statute requires aggrieved employees to file complaints with the EEOC before they are allowed to sue in federal court. The deadline for filing an ADEA charge varies depending on several factors.[67] Generally, a private sector employee must file a complaint with the EEOC within 180 days of the alleged discriminatory act. However, if the state where the alleged unlawful practice took place has an age discrimination law and a corresponding enforcement agency, then the time by which a claimant must file with the EEOC is extended to within 300 days of the alleged unlawful practice.[68]

After receiving a charge of unlawful discrimination, the EEOC conducts an investigation, and, if the claim is found to have merit, the agency may seek compliance with the statute through methods such as conciliation, conference, or persuasion.[69] Once 60 days have elapsed after the filing of a discrimination charge, then an ADEA plaintiff may file suit in federal court.[70] If the claimant decides to wait for a final determination from the EEOC, then he or she has 90 days to file suit in federal court once notified of the agency's final action.[71] It is important to note, however, that the EEOC has the authority to sue on behalf of an individual, in which case the individual's right to bring suit yields to the EEOC.[72]

Over the years, there has been some confusion over what constitutes a charge for purposes of triggering EEOC enforcement action. Under EEOC regulations, an ADEA complaint must, at a minimum: (1) be in writing, (2) name the prospective respondent, and (3) generally allege the discriminatory acts.[73] In addition to these regulatory requirements, EEOC policy states that a filing, in order to be deemed a charge, must contain a request for agency action to remedy the alleged age discrimination. The agency's position was validated by the Supreme Court in *Federal Express Corp. v. Holowecki*,[74] which held that a claimant's submission of an improper form was not fatal to her claim. According to the Court, "In addition to the information required by the regulations ... if a filing is to be deemed a charge it must be reasonably construed as a request for the agency to take remedial action to protect the employee's rights or otherwise settle a dispute between the employer and the employee."[75] Although this permissive standard may lead to a higher number of filings being deemed to be charges, the Court reasoned that giving inexperienced litigants the benefit of the doubt is more consistent with the remedial purpose of the ADEA.

Waiver and Arbitration

An employee may waive his rights under the ADEA if such waiver was knowing and voluntary.[76] In order to be considered knowing and voluntary, a waiver must comply with detailed requirements set forth in the statute.[77] A waiver given in settlement of a charge filed with the EOC or in a civil action is not considered knowing and voluntary unless the general requirements for a waiver are met and the individual has a reasonable opportunity to consider the settlement.[78] The person asserting validity of the waiver has the burden of proving that the waiver was knowing and voluntary. In addition, the waiver provision does not apply to the EEOC, nor may a waiver be used to interfere with an employee's right to file an age discrimination charge or participate in an EEOC investigation or proceeding.

On occasion, employers may, either deliberately or inadvertently, fail to comply with the ADEA's waiver requirements. In such cases, the courts must determine what effect the employee's acceptance of the statutorily deficient waiver has on the waiver's validity. In *Oubre v. Entergy Operations, Inc.*,[79] the employee received severance pay in return for waiving any claims against the employer, but the waiver did not fully comply with the ADEA's waiver requirements. The Supreme Court, reasoning that retention of severance benefits does not ratify a statutorily invalid waiver, held that the plaintiff did not have to return the money before bringing suit.[80]

A related issue is the effect of arbitration clauses on ADEA claims. The Court held in *Gilmer v. Interstate/Johnson Lane Corp.* that the ADEA does not preclude enforcement of a compulsory arbitration clause.[81] The plaintiff in *Gilmer* signed a registration application with the New York Stock Exchange (NYSE), as required by his employer. The application provided that the plaintiff would agree to arbitrate any claim or dispute that arose between him and Interstate. Gilmer filed an ADEA claim with the EEOC upon being fired at age 62. Interstate filed a motion to compel arbitration based on the application and the Federal Arbitration Act (FAA),[82] which was enacted to change the "longstanding judicial hostility to arbitration...."[83] Ultimately, the Court held that an ADEA claim may be subject to compulsory arbitration in accordance with an arbitration agreement contained in an employment contract.[84] Similarly, in 2009, the Court held that collective bargaining agreements that contain provisions requiring arbitration of ADEA claims are enforceable.[85]

Remedies

The remedies available under the ADEA are patterned on the Fair Labor Standards Act,[86] and may include injunctions, compelled employment, reinstatement, promotion, and back pay.[87] In addition, a willful violation of the act gives rise to liquidated damages, which are generally computed by doubling the amount awarded to the plaintiff.[88] According to the Supreme Court in *Trans World Air Lines v. Thurston*, "a violation of the Act [is] 'willful' if the employer knew or showed reckless disregard for the matter of whether its conduct was prohibited by the ADEA."[89] Upon proving a claim of age discrimination, a plaintiff is entitled to reasonable attorney's fees and costs.[90]

In addition, anyone who interferes with the EEOC's performance of its duties under the ADEA is subject to criminal penalties amounting to a fine or up to one year of prison, or both.[91]

III. Other Laws Prohibiting Age Discrimination

The ADEA is not the only legal remedy available to employees who have been subject to age discrimination. Other laws that may offer some degree of protection include the U.S. Constitution, federal statutes such as the Age Discrimination Act and the Congressional Accountability Act, and various state laws.

One alternative remedy to the ADEA is the U.S. Constitution. Although an employee seeking a remedy for age discrimination in employment may decide to file a constitutional challenge based on the Equal Protection Clause,[92] such a claim is unlikely to be successful. Because the Equal Protection Clause applies only to governmental entities, a plaintiff must show state action in order to establish such a claim. Moreover, the courts generally review legislation involving age classifications under a deferential standard of review, meaning that such legislation is highly likely to survive judicial scrutiny. For example, in *Gregory v. Ashcroft*,[93] the Supreme Court considered an Equal Protection Clause challenge to a Missouri law that required state judges to retire at age 70. Noting that "age is not a suspect classification under the Equal Protection Claus" "and that the plaintiffs did not "have a fundamental interest in serving as judges,"[94] the Court reviewed the claim under the deferential rational basis standard. Ultimately, the Court held that the state had a legitimate and rational basis for requiring retirement of their state judges to ensure the competency and efficacy of their judiciary.

Other remedial alternatives to the ADEA may be found in other federal statutes.[95] For example, the Age Discrimination Act prohibits discrimination on the basis of age in federally funded programs or activities.[96] Although each federal agency is responsible for enforcing compliance with respect to its funding recipients, the statute states that agencies are not authorized to take action against recipients with respect to their employment practices. However, it is possible, though not certain, that individuals may bring employment-related suits on their own. Meanwhile, as noted above, the Congressional Accountability Act applies several existing civil rights, labor, and workplace laws—including the ADEA—to employees of the legislative branch of the federal government.[97]

Finally, in addition to federal laws, most states have laws that prohibit age discrimination in private employment. The ADEA does not preempt such state laws, even when those laws are more stringent than the ADEA.[98]

End Notes

[1] 29 U.S.C. §§ 621 et seq.
[2] Id. at § 621.
[3] Id. at § 623.
[4] Reorg. Plan No. 1 of 1978, 92 Stat. 3781 (1978). See also 29 U.S.C. § 626(a).
[5] Id. at § 630(b).
[6] Id. at § 623(f)(1) and (h).
[7] Id. at § 623(h)(3).
[8] Id. at § 633a(a).
[9] 2 U.S.C. §§ 1301 et seq.
[10] 29 U.S.C. § 630. The Supreme Court in *EEOC v. Wyoming* declared constitutional the extension of the ADEA to state and local government employees as a valid use of Congress' authority under the Commerce Clause. 460 U.S. 226 (1983).
[11] 528 U.S. 62 (2000). See also, CRS Report RL30364, *Legal Issues Affecting the Right of State Employees to Bring Suit Under the Age Discrimination in Employment Act and Other Federal Labor Laws*, by Kimberly D. Jones.
[12] 29 U.S.C. § 630(d).
[13] Id. at § 630(e).
[14] Id. at § 630.
[15] Id. at § 631(a).

[16] 2 U.S.C. §§ 1301 et seq.

[17] 42 U.S.C. § 2000e-16.

[18] Although state court judges who are elected are clearly not covered by the ADEA, the status of appointed state court judges was less clear until the Supreme Court ruled in *Gregory v. Ashcroft* that such judges fall within the exception to the ADEA regarding "appointee on the policymaking level." 501 U.S. 452, 467 (1991).

[19] 29 U.S.C. § 631(c)(1).

[20] Id. at § 623(j).

[21] 5 U.S.C. § 8335.

[22] 29 U.S.C. at § 623(m).

[23] Id. at § 623(d). In *Robinson v. Shell Oil Co.*, a case involving Title VII of the Civil Rights Act, the Supreme Court held that ex-employees may sue for retaliation. 519 U.S. 337 (1997). Since the ADEA is closely modeled after Title VII, former employees appear to be protected from retaliation under the ADEA as well.

[24] 553 U.S. 474 (2008).

[25] Gen. Dynamics Land Sys. v. Cline, 540 U.S. 581 (2004).

[26] Id. at 584.

[27] O'Connor v. Consol. Coin Caterers Corp., 517 U.S. 308 (1996).

[28] 29 U.S.C. § 623(e).

[29] 29 C.F.R. § 1625.4(a).

[30] Id. at § 1625.4(b), 1625.5.

[31] Id. at § 1625.5.

[32] 29 U.S.C. § 623(f)(1).

[33] W. Air Lines v. Criswell, 472 U.S. 400, 414 (1985).

[34] Id.

[35] 29 U.S.C. § 623(f)(1).

[36] Id. at § 623(f)(3). In *McKennon v. Nashville Banner Pub. Co.*, the Court considered whether after-acquired evidence of employee misconduct would bar an ADEA claim. The Court held that after-acquired evidence, which, if discovered, would have led to the employee's discharge, does not bar an ADEA claim, but may reduce the amount of damages. 513 U.S. 352 (1995).

[37] Hazen Paper Co. v. Biggins, 507 U.S. 604 (1993). In *Biggins*, the plaintiff was fired weeks before he was scheduled to vest under his employer's pension plan, which allowed vesting after ten years of service. Although the Court held that firing an employee to prevent vesting is actionable under the Employees Retirement Income Security Act (ERISA), 29 U.S.C. § 1001 et seq., such firing "would not constitute discriminatory treatment on the basis of age," even though an employee's years of service may be highly correlated with age. Biggens, 507 U.S. at 612. However, the Court did not address the possibility of pension status being used as a proxy for age. If vesting were based on an employee's age, then firing an employee to avoid vesting could possibly result in liability under both the ADEA and ERISA. Id. at 613. Likewise, if an employer uses cost factors such as pension status or high salary as a proxy for age, then an ADEA violation may occur.

[38] 554 U.S. 135 (2008).

[39] 29 U.S.C. § 623(f)(2). See also, Trans World Airlines, Inc. v. Thurston, 469 U.S. 111 (1985). Bona fide is defined as a system or plan that is not being used to evade the purposes of the act.

[40] 29 U.S.C. § 623(f)(2)(B). In *Public Employees Retirement System of Ohio v. Betts*, the Court rejected the "equal benefits or equal costs" principle, holding that a bona fide employee benefit plan was permissible under the ADEA unless an employee could establish that adoption of the plan was a subterfuge for discrimination. 492 U.S. 158 (1989). The Older Workers Protection Act (P.L. 101-433), which amended the ADEA, restored the use of the "equal benefit or equal cost" principle after it had been invalidated by the Supreme Court in *Betts*.

[41] 220 F.3d 193 (3d Cir. 2000).

[42] 29 U.S.C. § 628.

[43] 72 FR 72938. When proposed, the EEOC regulation was challenged in court, and a permanent injunction blocking its implementation remained in effect for several years while the courts considered the issue. In 2007, the Third Circuit ruled that the EEOC's promulgation of the proposed rule was a reasonable exercise of the agency's exemption authority and lifted the injunction, thus allowing the EEOC to publish the final rule. AARP v. EEOC, 489 F.3d 558 (3d Cir. 2007), cert. denied, 128 S. Ct. 1733 (2008). For more information, see CRS Report RS21845, *Final Equal Employment Opportunity Commission (EEOC) Rules on Retiree Health Plans and the Age Discrimination in Employment Act (ADEA)*, by Jody Feder.

[44] Hazen Paper Co. v. Biggins, 507 U.S. 604 (1993). ("The disparate treatment theory is of course available under the ADEA, as the language of that statute makes clear.... By contrast, we have never decided whether a disparate impact theory of liability is available under the ADEA.") Id. at 609-610.

[45] 544 U.S. 228 (2005). For more information on this case, see CRS Report RS22170, *The Age Discrimination in Employment Act and Disparate Impact Claims: An Analysis of the Supreme Court's Ruling in Smith v. City of Jackson*, by Charles V. Dale and Jody Feder.

[46] Under the ADEA, plaintiffs may also bring a separate type of disparate treatment claim akin to Title VII "pattern or practice" suits, which involve habitual discriminatory actions on the part of the employer. Such class action claims carry a heavy evidentiary burden that follow different rules of proof. See, e.g., Int'l Bhd. of Teamsters v. United States, 431 U.S. 324 (1977).

[47] 411 U.S. 792 (1973); 450 U.S. 248 (1981).

[48] See, e.g., Trans World Airlines, Inc. v. Thurston, 469 U.S. 111 (1985).

[49] McDonnell Douglas, 411 U.S. 792, 802 (1973).

[50] St. Mary's Honor Center v. Hicks, 509 U.S. 502 (1993). In *Hicks*, the Supreme Court revisited the burden of proof scheme established by *McDonnell Douglas* and *Burdine*, holding that it is not enough for the plaintiff to show that the employer's proffered reason was false. The plaintiff must show that the employer's proffered reason is both false and that the employer's actions were motivated by discrimination. In *Reeves v. Sanderson Plumbing Products, Inc.*, the Court emphasized that "a plaintiff's prima facie case of age discrimination, combined with sufficient evidence to find that the employer's asserted justification for its action was false, may permit the trier of fact to conclude that the employer unlawfully discriminated," and the plaintiff need not always introduce additional and independent evidence of discrimination. 530 U.S. 133, 148-49 (2000).

[51] Burdine, 450 U.S. 248, 255-256 (1981).

[52] McDonnell Douglas, 411 U.S. at 802.

[53] The plaintiff must show that age was a motivating factor in the employer's decision, but does not have to show that it was the only factor. Kralman v. Illinois Dept. of Veteran's Affairs, 23 F.3d 150 (7th Cir. 1994), cert. denied, 513 U.S. 948 (1994).

[54] For example, in discharge cases, the Court has held that a prima facie case of age discrimination does not require a plaintiff to demonstrate that he or she was replaced by a person outside of the protected age class. Rather, replacement by someone who is substantially younger—even if that person is also a member of the protected class—may be sufficient for the plaintiff to demonstrate that he was replaced because of his age. O'Connor v. Consol. Coin Caterers Corp., 517 U.S. 308 (1996).

[55] 552 U.S. 379 (2008).

[56] Id. at 388.

[57] 490 U.S. 228 (1989).

[58] Once a "plaintiff shows that an impermissible motive played a motivating part in an adverse employment decision," the burden shifts to the employer "to show that it would have made the same decision in the absence of the unlawful motive." Id. at 250. If the employer fails to make this showing, it will be held liable. 42 U.S.C. §§ 2000e-2(m), 2000e-5(g)(2)(B).

[59] 129 S. Ct. 2343 (2009).

[60] Id. at 2352.

[61] For more information on the *Gross* case, see CRS Report R41279, *Mixed-Motive Claims Under the Age Discrimination in Employment Act: A Legal Analysis of the Supreme Court's Ruling in Gross v. FBL Financial Services, Inc.*, by Jody Feder.

[62] Smith v. City of Jackson, 544 U.S. 228 (2005).

[63] Id.

[64] 554 U.S. 84 (2008).

[65] Id.

[66] 29 U.S.C. § 626(a). The Department of Labor was originally responsible for enforcement of the ADEA. The authority was transferred to the EEOC in 1978 pursuant to Reorg. Plan No. 1 of 1978, 92 Stat. 3781 (1978).

[67] The filing procedures for federal employees vary somewhat from the filing procedures for private sector employees. Most notably, federal employees are required to seek resolution with the equal employment opportunity office at their respective agency prior to filing a charge of discrimination with the EEOC. 29 C.F.R. § 1614.105.

[68] 29 U.S.C. § 626(d). Additional filing deadlines apply to suits that are filed in state court. In states with age discrimination laws and an agency to administer such laws, the statute requires ADEA claimants to file suit in state court. Id. at § 633(b). The Supreme Court, in *Oscar Mayer & Co. v. Evans*, held that this provision requires claimants to pursue state claims prior to suing in federal court. However, the Court also held that this provision is satisfied by filing with the applicable state agency, that such charges do not need to be filed within the state law filing period, and that exhaustion of state remedies is not required before filing a complaint with the EEOC. 441 U.S. 750 (1979).

[69] 29 U.S.C. § 626(b).

[70] Id. at § 626(d). The statute gives private sector employees the right to a jury trial, but this right does not extend to federal employees. Lehman v. Nakshian, 453 U.S. 156 (1981).

[71] 29 U.S.C. § 626(e).

[72] Id. at § 626(c).

[73] 29 C.F.R. § 1626.6. The EEOC has a duty to accept charges that are submitted in person or over the telephone, and to put these charges in writing.

[74] 552 U.S. 389.

[75] Id. at 402.

[76] 29 U.S.C. § 626(f).

[77] Id. at § 626(f)(1). A waiver is knowing and voluntary if:

(A) the waiver is part of an agreement between the individual and the employer that is written in a manner calculated to be understood by such individual, or by the average individual eligible to participate;

(B) the waiver specifically refers to rights or claims arising under this chapter;

(C) the individual does not waive rights of claims that may arise after the date the waiver is executed;

(D) the individual waives rights or claims only in exchange for consideration in addition to anything of value to which the individual already is entitled;

(E) the individual is advised in writing to consult with an attorney prior to executing the agreement;

(F)(i) the individual is given a period of at least 21 days within which to consider the agreement; or

(ii) if a waiver is requested in connection with an exit incentive or other employment termination program offered to a group or class of employees, the individual is given a period of at least 45 days within which to consider the agreement;

(G) the agreement provides that for a period of at least 7 days following the execution of such agreement, the individual may revoke the agreement, and the agreement shall not become effective or enforceable until the revocation period has expired;

(H) if a waiver is requested in connection with an exit incentive or other employment termination program offered to a group or class of employees, the employer (at the commencement of the period specified in subparagraph (F)) informs the individual in writing in a manner calculated to be understood by the average individual eligible to participate, as to—

(i) any class, unit, or group of individuals covered by such programs, any eligibility factors for such program, and any time limits applicable to such program; and

(ii) the job titles and ages of all individuals eligible or selected for the program, and the ages of all individuals in the same job classification or organizational unit who are not eligible or selected for the program.

[78] Id. at § 626(f)(2).

[79] 522 U.S. 422 (1998).

[80] Id. at 428. An employer, however, may be entitled to deduct the original settlement amount from any damages awarded in a subsequent lawsuit.

[81] 500 U.S. 20 (1990).

[82] 9 U.S.C. §§ 1 et seq.

[83] Gilmer, 500 U.S. at 24. Courts are less likely to honor arbitration agreements contained in a collective bargaining agreement. See, e.g., Alexander v. Gardner-Denver Co., 415 U.S. 36 (1974).

[84] Gilmer, 500 U.S. at 23.

[85] 14 Penn Plaza LLC v. Pyett, 129 S. Ct. 1456 (2009).

[86] 29 U.S.C. § 626(b).

[87] Id. at § 216(b).

[88] Id. at § 626(b). Compensatory and punitive damages are not available under the ADEA.

[89] 469 U.S. 111, 126 (1985).

[90] 29 U.S.C. § 216(b).

[91] Id. at § 629.

[92] U.S. Const. amend. XIV, § 1. The Equal Protection Clause states in part, "[n]o state shall ... deny to any person within its jurisdiction the equal protection of the laws."

[93] 501 U.S. 452 (1991).

[94] Id. at 470.

[95] It is unclear whether plaintiffs may bring age discrimination in employment claims under certain provisions of the Reconstruction Statutes, namely 42 U.S.C. § 1983 or 42 U.S.C. § 1985.

[96] 42 U.S.C. §§ 6101 et seq.

[97] 2 U.S.C. §§ 1301 et seq.

[98] 29 U.S.C. § 633(a).

INDEX

A

B

C

D

E

F

G

H

I

J

Q

R

S